THE AVERAGE INDIAN MALE

BY THE SAME AUTHOR

'A laugh riot.' – *Mail Today*

'(Cyrus) at his hilarious best.' – *The Times of India*

'Laced with humour, tongue-in-cheek one liners and witty narration.' – *The Asian Age*

THE AVERAGE INDIAN MALE

Cyrus Broacha

RANDOM HOUSE INDIA

Published by Random House India in 2011

1

Copyright © Cyrus Broacha 2011

Random House Publishers India Private Limited
Windsor IT Park, 7th Floor, Tower-B,
A-1, Sector-125, Noida 201301, UP

Random House Group Limited
20 Vauxhall Bridge Road
London SW1V 2SA, UK

978-81-8400-160-0

Typeset in Weiss by Jojy Philip

Printed and bound in India by Replika Press

Contents

Book One: Letters from the Anguished Soul and Other Narratives

Book Two: The Incoherent Thoughts of an Average Indian Male

Foreword

I have not read this book. I have no intention of reading it either, and I have a very good reason for it. After having known the author from soup to nuts for over 20 years, there is nothing in this book that I have not heard straight from this horse before.

The content in this collection of essays is based on the author being an astute snoop of human behaviour, an impossible critic, complainer, fault-finder, grumbler, and moaner about most things living and male.

For years I have been a listener to his critique, whether in the passenger seat of a car, in a queue at an airport, in the dressing room of the Bombay Gymkhana, at the anchor desk of a news studio, or the most spastic of all places and situations including a booming voice mixed with the sound of a flush from behind the closed door of a public toilet. His observations often range from being clever, blithe, facetious to sometimes puerile, volatile, and pompous. But when he puts pen to paper and spews his venom in print, it is nothing short of pure wit and uproarious to read. This I can say without even reading the book.

The book promises to take you through a minefield of traits of the average Indian male. Traits that we all may have noticed but failed to register. Be it the way we dress, the way we hold hands, scratch our groins in public, or invade personal space. Broacha watches, notes, and spins them into prose that is an entertaining almanac. His writing style is 'him'. He writes pretty much the way he speaks, and I daresay, seemingly without much thought. But then when you have been thinking about all this all your life, do you really need to think about all this, all over again when you sit to put it down? I don't think so.

This is Cyrus Broacha's second book. Though he continues to embrace a potent career as a stand-up comedian, television anchor, and theatre actor, Broacha's propensity remains the written word. He has uninterruptedly for over fifteen years remained a columnist for some national publication or the other. To date he writes at least three columns a week. Self admittedly, writing gives Broacha more joy than standing in front of a camera, donning make-up, or wearing a suit to entertain a crowd. He still uses pen and paper and illegibly scribbles in a variety of notepads in a font that only his mother and aunt can decipher and that his wife gave up on long ago. This is a compilation of all that chicken scratch.

I will someday get down to reading this book, but that should not discourage you from doing so. That's because if you are an Indian male, you feature in this book. If you are an Indian female, your father, brother, husband, and all your male friends and relatives are characters here. I am sure some of you will recognise yourselves in this book as most of us would. So, if it says anywhere in the book that any resemblance to real persons, living or dead, is purely coincidental and unintentional, don't believe it.

KUNAL VIJAYAKAR

Introduction

To fully understand the Indian male and, more importantly, to further complicate the issue, this book is structured into seven books—five of the seven books, we immediately donated to charity. Thus, we are now stuck with two books disguised as one book, purely for tax purposes. This one book must now be referred to in the plural. Hence, a conversation you have with your mother about this book would go as such.

You: Hey, mom, would you like to read Cyrus Broacha's books called *The Average Indian Male*?

Mom: Of course not. Have I lost my marbles?

You: Are you sure?

Mom: My answer is no and no. No for each book that makes up the books.

Now that everything is partly clear, let me assure you that the two books have different processes. Book One contains letters from various anguished people thirsty for answers, which is interspersed with witty and profound observations from… err…me. These, dear reader, I must warn you, are sometimes connected and sometimes don't make any sense at all. But they are of immense value and can be life-altering if you follow the advice given. Book Two lists my experiences about being around and occasionally being the average Indian male and sometimes throws in a list of stories that offer amazing weekend discounts on any large purchases. The intention again is to thoroughly confuse you, dear reader. That said, let's get on with the business of the book, sorry books.

Before we start with Book One we need to know something about the author, namely…err…me, who I'm told, probably by himself, is very much an average Indian male, with a propensity to go below average whenever and wherever possible.

Here are his statistics. He was born…err…many years ago. In some cultures, he may be considered fat, and in the rest very fat. Since his toes aren't detachable, he has never actually touched them. No one else has actually touched them either. No one else has ever evinced the slightest interest in touching them. He can swim normally one full length, after which he has to be fished out of the water, and given tremendous amounts of oxygen. 'Charity begins at home', says the sign in every orphanage, so let's look into the author's own life to get our first insight into that machine-like beast known as the average Indian male.

I first became acquainted with the average Indian male through my uncles, Phiroze and Phillip. Of course my father himself is largely male, but since he is my father, it's difficult to be objective. With uncles you get that little space which makes all the difference. My uncle Phiroze is my father's elder brother. At age four, he gave me my most favourite present—a 300-year-old dumbbell, which is roughly 15 pounds in weight. As a 4-year-old, one doesn't really know one's Ronnie Coleman from one's Jay Cutler. Or one's chin-up from one's Romanian dead-lift. So I did the three things that all 4-year-olds will do when confronted with an old rusty dumbbell for the first time:

a) sat on it
b) flung it at my uncle
c) tried to eat it

My uncle Phiroze, of course, continued to make a lasting impression as he stood there explaining the importance of balance and feet position before

xiv

entering into a 500 pound squat. Phiroze's stocky frame, balding scalp, and large forearms gave me an insight into maleness. Till the age of 27, I thought all males would eventually look like my uncle Phiroze. Then I saw my friend's grandmom, Freny Aunty, and she had the same look (except of course for her bigger forearms), and my male stereotype was shattered, temporarily.

My mother's brother Phillip was another macho man, or like we Catholics like to say, a 'Machado' man. Phillip didn't believe in buttons. To be sure, I don't know if he even knew about the existence of buttons. His shirt, always open, revealed his bare chest, and his entire gold collection. When he'd take me for a spin on his Tiger Triumph, I'd try to match up to him. Sitting pillion, I'd remove a button. I'd have removed more, but my T-shirts generally only ever had the one button. At the age of 7, I was a poor man's Phillip or as the saying goes, a 'minor Machado'. Phillip and Phiroze were the opening batsmen, but the middle order was packed with plenty of Indian males…average Indian males that is.

Before we get into a complex biopsy of the subject, we need to have a physical and geographical grounding of the very same subject. Keep the subject's feet on terra firma, if you will, thereby presenting a strong visual of the subject which will stay in the readers' mind through the length or breadth of the book. The latter, of course, will come in handy when this book is translated into Persian.

After all, it is morally wrong and completely unjustified to presume that all our readers are familiar with the average Indian male. I mean, one doesn't write a book about, say, the duck-billed platypus without at least one picture of the platypus itself. It is even worse to assume that a book on the average Indian male will be read by the average Indian male. I mean, it's not like the book on the white tiger was read exclusively by white tigers! In fact, at the time of this book going into print, you can have it on good record that not a single white tiger would have actually read the book on the damned white tiger. So before you read the rest of this book, commit to memory the following details about our subject:

a) Name: Average Indian male
b) Latin Name: Manush, purush, aam aadmi, Bunty
c) Found: From Kashmir in the North to Kanyakumari in the South, from Bengal in the East to the Rann of Kutch in the West.

Also, occasionally spotted in Goa and Pondicherry, but mostly at night. Other known habitats include USA, Australia, Canada, East Africa, Southhall, Houston, and the southern tip of Paraguay. Two sightings of the average Indian male have also occurred in East Timor, but clearly on the more western part

d) Height: Generally as much as 5 feet 7 (if measured by himself)

e) Coat: Generally too big for him

f) Colour: Normally seen in grayish pants with large brown shirt with a gunjee—also known as a vest—inside; it is what defines him the most

g) Other characteristics: Sweats a lot, and on many occasions, breathes heavily

h) Attributes include: Digging his nose in public, scratching his privates, wearing belts which don't match his shoes, and an extremely strong, unnatural affection for his mother

i) Drawbacks: Punctuality and commitment. As can be exemplified by many volunteers who were supposed to have been researched for this book. Most of them didn't come in time for the sessions and the rest didn't want to commit to any statement on record

j) Weight: 45 percent more after marriage. The average Indian male has this huge ability to put on weight only on his stomach area, completely ignoring his other parts in totality

k) Most likely cause of death: Traffic.

Now that we are acquainted with the said subject, let us all go on with our social commentary in the best possible way, that is, without the subject's permission.

BOOK ONE

Letters from the Anguished Soul and Other Narratives

The following letters are 100 percent authentic. How do you know they are authentic? Well, because I've touched the letters...most of them, anyhow. And not in an unbecoming way. These letters are the last shreds of altruism to be found in the modern world. As we have progressed into this information age (the last hundred years have given us the five greatest inventions of all time— the geyser, the air-conditioner, the toaster, the telephone, and the karaoke machine), our humanity is the one quality that seems to be challenged.

These letters are proof (if any is needed) that all is not lost, and there are some champions of compassion, some sultans of sensitivity, some badshahs of...okay, you got me, I can't find a suitable word to match with badshah, so let's just move on to the first letter. And remember, if you haven't written in, and you feel you too can help, well it's...err...too late.

Apna haath jagganath

Dear Cyrus,

I spent two beautiful months in your beloved country, out of which, half the time I was in Mumbai and Delhi. The other half, unfortunately, I was in the toilet. The one strong memory I have of both Mumbai and Delhi is that most of the men roam around holding each other's hand. My question to you, sir, is—does this mean they are all homosexuals?

As a practicing homosexual myself, who doesn't get that much time to practice any more, I'm intrigued. By the way, are you gay as well?
Lots of extra love and kisses (everywhere),
Havel Rafael Hernandez,
Madrid, Spain.

Dear Havel Rafael Hernandez,

Let me answer your last query first. Up to the time of reading your letter, I can clearly say that I'm not gay, although definitely not for want of trying. But, as you know, gay men are attracted to the most hygienic and orderly folk. I fail on all these counts. At the three gay parties I've attended, I was mistaken for a member of the catering staff. Every single time. Institutionalized rejection from a variety of women day after day, month after month, year after year, has forced me, however, to keep my options open.

Regarding the issue of Indian men holding hands, are such persons practicing homosexuals? The answer to this is pretty straight forward. Yes and no. Yes, they are practicing homosexuals and no, they are not practicing homosexuals.

Now this statement of mine may initially flabbergast you. Mainly because it is in English and you speak Spanish, and the whole world knows there is no word for 'flabbergast' in the Spanish language. However, allow me to (as you Spainiards say) elucidate.

Homosexuality in India is as old as the hills, which in our case are the Nilgiris. It has been around from time immemorial when God was keen on experimenting with Adam and a variety

4

of his friends; keep in mind that none of them at that time was named Eve. In the modern Indian context, men hold hands for a variety of reasons, which are uniquely native to only India. Some of these reasons are:

a) men who are so dazed after interacting with their alpha females that they need the steadying clasp of a friend just to help soothe their highly rattled nerves

b) men who are blind and, hence, use a friend's hand as their guide

c) men who are extremely malnourished—India has the most number of extremely ectomorphic males found in the world. Such men need a stronger companion to hold them down in case they defy gravity. This also explains why there are a higher number of hand–holding cases in Marine Drive in Mumbai and India Gate in Delhi, as these places are notorious for India's strongest gusts of wind

d) men who are injured on their wrists and are using a companion's hand to hold the appliance in place

e) rich men who are dysfunctionally lazy and employ attendants to move their limbs for them

5

f) men who are feeling cold, especially on their hands but have forgotten to wear a coat with pockets

g) synchronized swimmers

h) dancers at a rehearsal

i) policemen and criminals. In India, in an effort to safeguard the waning steel deposits, the government has banned steel handcuffs and so criminals are escorted by hand, literally

j) men who, missing a digit or two from their hand, don't want attention drawn to the fact

k) members of the opposition party, the BJP, who are trying to discredit and cover the Congress's grand symbol—the hand

l) and lastly, men who are practicing homosexuals.

Our research tells us that the percentage of men holding hands who really are gay is about 17.6 percent. So, again, in India, are men who hold hands practicing homosexuals? The answer is a simple yes and no.

P.S.: Havel Rafael Hernandez, in India we have another grand tradition of holding, clasping, and sometimes tugging madly at our elder's feet. This is done both to show respect and improve flexibility simultaneously. So keep in mind that ours is a

6

culture that prides itself on grabbing, limb-holding, touching, and caressing. It is as old as the Vedas, the Puranas, and Sachin Tendulkar's tennis elbow.

Dearest Havel, if on your next visit you see anyone grab at a hand or a foot, please only react if the said hand or foot has been severed from the body.

Thanks for writing.

Your friend,

Cyrus.

Lift kara de

Dear Cyrus,

I have just moved to Mumbai from Meerut to attend classes at S.P. Jain. For the uninformed, S.P. Jain is no longer a person, but is, indeed, a management school. During my school break I plan to do an internship with a bank at Nariman Point. For the uninformed, Nariman, which today is just a point, used to, in days gone by, be a person.

In Meerut, most people are rather forthcoming and friendly. The few who are not, are easy to spot as they are constantly shooting at you. You may not know this, but there are no lifts in Meerut. There is a lift in my new office building and I am rather excited about using it all the way up to the sixteenth floor (despite my office being situated on the lowly third floor). I'm told that the lift is the ultimate vehicle for socializing in big cities.

Can you please guide me on lift culture? Or rather, 'lift couture'?

Yours sincerely,

Arvind Vaibhav,

Meerut.

(enclosed is a picture of a list, so you can refrequent yourself with the machine).

Dear Arvind,

Kudos to you on your fabulous question! The media, as well as the government, is wasting too much time and attention on inconsequential things such as nuclear proliferation, tourism, communalism, Naxalite insurgency, and drought. They would serve our society much better if they addressed the smaller and more everyday problems of our society, such as the lift. These small things and our understanding of them, can make or break, and launch, many unbelievable opportunities and occasionally, body posture.

The first thing you must notice about your lift is whether it has bars or sealed doors. If it has sealed doors, you must dress up for it. Suits, chiffon saris and the like. If it has bars, you must take great care to keep your fingers out of the bars when the lift

9

is in motion. Apparently this can lead to a very painful outcome, and not just for the lift.

The next thing you must notice about the lift is whether it has a queue. If it does, always stand at the back of the queue in order to enjoy Newton's third law of motion (every action has an equal and opposite reaction) better. By standing at the end of the queue, you will get into the lift last but most importantly, you will exit the lift first.

Lift travellers will come in two types—the majority will avoid eye contact, and stare at the floor like they are looking for some lost change. Some may hum or sing tunelessly in a loony manner, while they simultaneously try to look savvy, and others will talk loudly into a cell phone. If you encounter the latter, it will serve you well to surreptitiously persuade the gentleman concerned to grasp the bars of the lift door with his free hand. To maximize the effect, try and ensure that this is done when the lift is in motion. You will find an exceeding amount of support for this action among the other lift users.

Now this brings me to the most important piece of equipment in the lift—the mirror. Generally, across the world, each lift traveller is entitled to 2.2 seconds with the mirror. Sadly, we Indians, unused to orderly behaviour, abuse this privilege and try to extend our mirror invitation to well over the allotted time. In Mumbai, there have been recorded instances of one lift traveller hogging the mirror for up to as much as 38 seconds in an overcrowded lift. One gentleman was actually lynched by an irate lift mob as he neatly combed his hair in front of the mirror for 3 minutes and 44 seconds. To be fair to him though, Calcutta, that morning, was experiencing heavy fog, and visibility was extremely poor.

However, as unpopular as the cell phone user and mirror hogger are, the one that is usually most detested is the liftman.

This man has to have the world's second worst job description after, of course, a proctologist. But unlike a proctologist, a liftman can't even get some variety by changing lifts. Highly educated professors don't get lured to this post, which explains why very few MBAs, engineers, and others are liftmen. A liftman's job description, as spelt out by the World Liftman's Almanac, is as follows:

a) open door
b) close door
c) press button
d) repeat.

Due to the repetitive nature of this work, four things happen:

11

a) he develops a tennis elbow
b) his unutilized arm stops functioning
c) when he reaches his own home he always uses the stairs and
d) he never wears shirts with buttons.

To top it all, he has to wear the same outfit every single day at work. While this may be quite something for 'Batman', it doesn't work so well for 'Liftman'. So avoid communicating with this friendly, really, really poor man's superhero.

Lastly, remember there is great scope for romance in a lift. I met my wife in a lift. She used to go to the fifth floor and I to the fourth floor, and we both made sure we just dropped her husband off on the third.

P.S.: Arvind, lifts in our country are overcrowded. The only way to get through the pushing, rubbing, jostling, and caressing is to actually enjoy it. Just make sure you don't enjoy it too much.

12

Although India is divided into thousands of states, for the purpose of the following study I am dividing this huge country into five zones—the north, south, west, east, and a certain central zone. The central zone will consist of all the states that we've forgotten to list in the first four zones. Obviously this is a very sensitive subject and one must tread carefully. Keeping this in mind, I have created a two-way system listing the good and bad points of each participant, hopefully creating a perfect and harmonious balance, and the most definitive mini guidebook on the average Indian male.

The North Zone Male

Good point:
   a) they are from the north.

Bad points:
   a) they indulge in the most body touching among all five zones. This includes your body as well as their own
   b) public spitting is a registered sport in the north, so tread carefully if you are a tourist in these parts. You don't want to get caught in the crossfire of betel nut juice or phlegm
   c) digestive sounds such as a good burp and a pant-ripping fart are encouraged publicly.

Also, the louder the sound, the more of a man you are

d) giving seating space to ladies in buses is not considered good manners. Pushing old ladies off buses is worthy of praise

e) staring or ogling at a woman's exposed body part is the favourite way to kill time. Males here can stare for days on end, braving thunder and dust storms

f) a problem, any problem, is always solved by a loud voice and the repeated question of 'do you know who I am?', even if he has only just rammed his car into yours, and you are meeting him for the very first time. If you have a poor larynx then you may not enter the north zone

g) and above all, the north male is always, always right.

The South Zone Male

Good point:

a) they are from the south, more importantly they are not from the north, Thank God!

Bad points:

a) although polite, they will secretly revile you

b) there is an unshakeable belief that outside the south, intellectual capacity is seriously challenged. This intellectual capacity may diminish the further north you go. The south male will desperately look down on you if you are not from the south

c) they pride themselves as highly hygienic, which means that when they travel through the rest of India, their luggage consists of innumerable bars of soap and flower patterned towels and thousands of kilos of powder

d) if you are a tourist in the south, and you have just been mugged or your bag has been snatched, be assured that you will never ever catch the thief, even if you did get a good handful of his hair. It's a hundred percent guarantee that he will slip away because of the copious amounts of hair oil he has applied on his hair, keeping him slick and out of prison

e) the south zone is also said to be the most insular of all the zones, that is, you can't take the south out of the south zone.

The East Zone Male

Good point:

a) they are from the east...sometimes.

Bad points:

a) the east zone male is the laziest. There is a

15

story of two east zone farmers who refused to leave their house during their siesta even when their house was on fire

b) do you know why the east zone has the least number of bridges and connecting roads? It's because they can't fund anyone to build them and then who the hell is going to travel on them anyway

c) the east zone male is the master of the excuse. He even has an excuse for his excuse. For example Satyajit says, 'Sorry, ma'am, I can't carry your bag because I'm protecting my back. If my back goes out again, how will I help at the Little Hearts Orphanage next week?' There are more excuses available per day in the east zone than in the rest of the world put together

d) since excuses reign, the noise level in the east zone exceeds even that of the north zone. When compared with the east zone, the south zone is often called a silent zone

e) all the penury is still blamed on Robert Clive and East India Company

f) they still can't believe Siraj Ud Daula lost the Battle of Plassey because it was fought early in the morning. Too bloody early, in fact.

The West Zone Male

Good point:

a) they are from the west, and they haven't heard of the other zones.

Bad points:

a) the West zone male is a perfect amalgamation of the first three zones

b) they indulge in enough body touching and public spitting to show a clear northern influence. They also have the disdain and mistrust of others, which comes from the southern comfort

c) they can also almost match excuses and argue as directly, if incessantly, with their eastern counterparts. This is primarily because the western zone is the most porous zone with the most number of citizens who are a visiting faculty from other zones and who ultimately never leave.

that leaves us with the Central Zone Males

Good point:

a) there aren't any. None discovered so far.

Bad points:

a) too many to mention

b) also a very controversial zone in itself, as no one knows who to include in it. The theory

17

is that the weakest males from each of the other zones gets relegated into this central zone. Thus, they generally inherit the worst of the worst, year after year. The proof of the central zone's status is seen in the fact that it is the last place any member of the other four zones would opt to be transferred to.

I hope this highly researched and complex account helps you. If you're an Indian male check your category, and see how you can improve yourself. If you're a northern male, you know there's no room for improvement and that you're doomed. If you're a southern male, you really hope the others can improve. Eastern males obviously may defer any attempts for improvement to tomorrow. And western males may avail of any of the three options. As for central zone males...err...the truth is that in some situations, there is nothing anyone can do; and between you and me prayer, not only is highly overrated but also futile and a complete waste of time.

ᗯᗯ

Ungli dikhao

Dear Arvind Khurana,

I am quite sick of you. If I had to find two words in the whole of the English language that would most aptly describe you, those two words would be 'you suck!' You absolutely and completely suck. I have tolerated all your bad habits, your bad temper, and your innate chauvinism, but I won't, I just won't tolerate your nails. Your filthy, uncut, shapeless, gargantuan nails!

In particular, I speak of three nails which are the worst offenders. The thumb nail on your right hand, which has grown perpendicular to your thumb when it is held straight up. Normally this alone would not be such a bad thing, but a length of three and a half inches? In a month or so it'll qualify as an extra limb. Then, next to it, you have a nail on your forefinger that's a complete opposite of Newton's Law of Gravity, as it gravitates downwards forming a sort of question mark that's perpetually descending. One can't help wondering if foreign tourists will pay money to view it, as they do for the Taj Mahal in Agra (which by the way is also descending downwards at a rapid pace).

But dear Arvind, both these aforementioned nails pale in comparison to what you carry on the little finger of your left hand. A nail that bifurcates into two nails, which then travel in opposite directions, resulting in a strange rectangular shape. But that's not all. You then have the audacity to use that offensive digit to dig your ear in public!

You offensive, oily little man, nothing you can say in your defence will make any difference to me, as this is not a reconciliatory letter. This is a letter of dismissal. So while you can keep your nails, Arvind Khurana, I won't be keeping you.
Liza Cherian.

Dear Liza,

I have been called many terrible things in my life such as buffoon, moron, Ashlokh (German), and far worse than all his—uncle. However, I have never yet been called Arvind. Let me tell you why. Mainly because I'm not an Arvind and I've never been an Arvind. In fact, none of my friends are called

20

Arvind. Although one of my friend's stepfather may have been an Arvind, but we're still unsure about it. However, since this letter has accidentally reached me, I'll pretend I'm an Arvind.

Let me explain to you, dear Liza, as to why we men, specifically Indian men, like to grow our finger nails. Our reasons are different from the Italians, who grow their finger nails largely because they forget to cut them. Traditionally, among the old Indian texts such as the Puranas, the Upanishads, and even the early Chetan Bhagat books, finger nails were a sign of virility. For instance, in Samudragupta's court there existed a warrior prince, Asambhav, who had finger nails longer than the actual length of his fingers. Asambhav also had five official wives and 3,207 concubines. His insatiable appetite was directly linked to the length of his finger nails, and may I add, absolutely nothing else. Of course, the flip side to all this was pretty grim. By the age of 38, he had disfigured 577 of his female admirers and decapitated twenty-seven more. Only 10 percent of these casualties were deliberate. The rest were all caused by the inability to reign in the fingernails. Nails of gigantic lengths that seemed to take a life of their own when they entered the harem. Asambhav himself died in a freak accident, a result

21

of him digging his nose in a particularly famous manner one fine day. By the time they surgically removed the nail from the nostril, Asambhav had already been dead for five and a half hours.

Legend has it that those with extremely long fingernails are direct descendents of Asambhav, who, by the way, also invented the term 'hit the nail on the head' as he evidenced from the twenty-seven dead concubines.

What I'm trying to say, Liza, is that long, winding fingernails are a badge of honour. Maybe instead of flying into a rage, you could first see the story from the other side for a change.

If, however, you are still not convinced of the veracity and necessity of long nails, let me just remind you that quite frankly, I'm not Arvind, and that I don't know anyone called Arvind, except my friend's stepfather who may or may not have been an Arvind.
Yours faithfully,
Not Arvind Khurana.

P.S.: If at all this answer still does't satisfy you, let me recommend the one word that always successfully rhymes with love—'GLOVE' as a solution to your problem.

22

Mere paas maa hai

Dear Sir,

My name is Smita Khanna. I got married to my fiancé, Tarun, last month. Although he's perfectly nice, except for the pimples, he seems obsessed with his mother. Our bedroom has eleven pictures in it, and out of these, ten are of his mother. The eleventh? Well, that's a picture of his mother's mother, his grandmother!

The other day I bought tickets for a movie, but he declined saying his mother thinks he's very tired and that he should sleep early. Yesterday as she lay sleeping, I was about to smother her with a pillow, but I decided otherwise, as he was sitting right there fanning her with my favourite magazine (*Cosmopolitan*). Help, I'm turning homicidal!!!
Smita.

Dear Smita,

I'm amazed that someone, anyone, could actually use *Cosmo* as a fan. I find it too heavy on the wrist, and frankly I stick to *India Today*, although, my first preference would be the *Time*. However, *India Today* is far cheaper and I don't speak metaphorically. Now, Smita my girl, your problem unfortunately is extremely common and this situation you find yourself in has more to do with the average Indian mother, than the average Indian male. (Although rarely they do become one—the same thing.)

In other cultures, the Indian mother is also known as the 'suffocator'. Among mothers all over the world, there is no parallel to the Indian mother. The reason for this is a mistaken understanding of Chapter 8, Page 4 of the Rig Veda (the new edition; Random House). Here a mother's role is described as one who must mother her son from start to finish. The actual translation from the original Prakrit should read 'a mother's role is to mother a child a lot in the start and a little in the finish'. Note the word used is 'child' as against 'male child', and the mother's role is defined as great in infancy and in case she outlives her son, a little comfort towards the end.

However, because of this misreading or misinterpretation, Indian mothers are obsessed

24

with their sons, and can't stop themselves from suffocating the child with love and attention. This is all very well until the child turns 42, and then when she still towels him off after a swim, it can be socially quite damaging.

These acts of mothering tend to be more dangerous once the social dynamics get grounded by the arrival of a daughter-in-law. Among the most aggressive acts recorded by the WWF (Worldwide Wife Federation), these are the most offensive:

a) hand-feeding the son in the presence of the daughter-in-law. This is often done while maintaining eye-contact with the daughter-in-law at all times during the feeding

b) massaging the forehead and temples of the son after a hard day's work

c) at the dinner table, providing fresh rotis... only for the son

d) bathing the son

e) filing his nails

f) choosing and laying out his clothes

g) waxing his legs

h) and the most aggressive act of all, asking him, 'How was your day?'

Smita, sadly there is not much one can do except to rectify the translation of the Rig Veda (Prakrit version) with immediate effect. But even after we

25

do that, this malady may take years to reverse, as Prakrit is a language which you will discover has only three vowels in total.

Yet don't lose all hope merely over some photographs. A simple blue muslin cloth will do the job, without compromising on the room's aesthetic appeal. And oh yes, there is one way to teach your husband and mother-in-law a lesson. A lesson that's so hard they'll soon be reeling. It's a solution that's hardly original and has been tried before. But don't let that stop you. Just go ahead and have a son of your own, and if your mother-in-law is still around when he's 42, we'll see who'll be doing the bathing then.

Yours sincerely,
Cyrus.

P.S.: Smita, please don't take the extreme step of adding a moustache to your mother-in-law's photograph. This sort of thing usually misfires, as a moustache on a woman of a certain vintage can in actuality be quite fetching as I often tell my wife.

26

India is a unique country.

We have the largest number of rivers and seas with the least amount of swimmers per square metre of water. We have the second highest number of wild animals and parliamentarians in the world. Yet 91 percent of our population has never actually seen an elephant and 93 percent of our population is under the impression that the Home Minister is in charge of housing. 57.7 percent of Indians are vegetarians, yet 88.3 percent of the vegetarian segment is scared of dogs, cats, and pigeons. Most of them, in fact, have only interacted with one animal throughout their entire adult life—lice.

When it comes to marital relations, we are even more unique. In the Western world, marriages break up over things such as incompatibility, lack of a second television set, or the inability to share one's innerwear with one another. In India, none of these reasons are valid. In fact, here marriages break up over one and only one reason.

Hot chappatis.

A typical Western family sits down for dinner together. The lady of the house then puts out all the assorted food on the table in one go, settles down with her appetizer, and talks to her family, conversation which normally consists of her herding and belittling her spouse about his lack

27

of drive in front of the children. Dinner is then consumed in one shot. Nobody gets up during the meal, not even if war is declared, which happens, by the way, far too often in the Western world, especially on weekends.

In India, the wife's job description is a little different. The wife's job is absolutely parallel to a trampoline artist's. She has to bounce around the dinner table attending to each and every person's need. The average household in middle class India seats seven people for dinner. This is made up of her husband, the two children Bunty and Neha, the dada and dadima, and the perennial houseguest Dr Sen Gupta. The wife, let's call her Jyotsna aunty, now has to cater to all seven at breakneck speed. She has to jump from chair to chair like a bunny rabbit on speed, serving hot food on each person's plate.

Her husband Nirmal, being a BP patient, has to have his food cooked with Tata low sodium salt. This of course won't do for his parents. His dad likes his food the old fashioned Indian way—swimming in oil, ghee, and salt from the middle ages. Dadima, on the other hand, can't eat solid food anymore since she recently had her teeth relaid. Jyotsna aunty has to quickly cough up some soup and mashed vegetables for her. Young

28

Bunty is a paneer freak and eats paneer in different forms morning, noon, and night. Paneer is made separately only for him. In fact, 72 percent of Bunty is now paneer. Neha, all of 13, is watching her figure so she's on a pure vegetarian diet of boiled pulses without any carbs. Dr Sen Gupta on the other hand, is a pure non-vegetarian, who alone is responsible for the sudden disappearance of 50 percent of all marine life in the Indian Ocean. A separate fish curry, with clams on the side, is made for him, as he completes his seventh year of 'just visiting'. But what does all this have to do with hot chapattis, I can hear you scream? The answer, dear reader, is everything.

You see, in between the low sodium meal, the old fashioned meal, the special broth, the paneer exclusive, the pure pulses extravaganza, and the fish curry rice and clams; in between the sabzi, the salad, the papad, the fruit, and the sweet dish; in between the cucumber, the pickle, the aamias, and the falooda, poor Jyotsna aunty has to make one and a half million dishes to bring out just one fresh, hot chapatti every forty-five seconds.

There is not one Indian male, alive or dead, vegetarian or non-vegetarian, married, single, or divorced, who doesn't insist on fresh, hot chapattis. His wife can be ugly, disinterested, disrespectful,

29

and socially awkward, but as long as she delivers fresh, piping hot chapattis one at a time, the marriage will last. The converse also is true. She may be hot as hell, but with one cold chapatti the union will close faster than an American bank. This is why Indian mothers insist their boys shouldn't marry foreigners. It's got nothing to do with race, geography, or culture. It's just about the fresh, hot chapatti.

30

The long and short of Indian pants

Hello Cyrus,

I'm writing in for a peculiar reason. In fact, I'm a little embarrassed.

First, a little about myself. I was born in Poland to parents who said they were Polish, but in their defence, never to me. My father was a diplomat, so he lived for a considerable time in Latvia, Peru, the Slovak Republic, Honolulu, and Ghana. My first husband was Chinese, though now he's defected to Taiwan. My second husband, a South African, went to study Orangutans in Borneo and never returned. I have been with men of many cultures and races, and recently I started dating an Indian gentleman by the name of Dibakar Goswami. His friends call him DG, his mother calls him Dilu, and I call him Dibakar Goswami. That is because

I don't believe in wasting names. Names, after all, are there for a reason. That is also why I call it the United States of America instead of just the States and the erstwhile USSR that instead of 'that neighbouring country'.

Now back to my peculiar dilemma. My boyfriend is really sweet and considerate, but in bed, and especially on Sundays, I've noticed one strange feature. He has spaghetti legs. His legs are thin as straws. He normally wears baggy trousers, so you can't quite tell, but when he removes them, it's like a magician performing a trick—his legs just disappear. I'm so embarrassed by his skinny legs that I've given up going swimming with him. I refuse to get married to a man who is propped up by a pair of candles. When I confronted him about his inadequacies, he blamed it on Indian genetics. Now here is my peculiar question, dear sir, is it true that all Indian men have spindly legs?
Ms Jana Pedrowski Chang Boermann.

Dear Ms Jana Pedrowski Chang Boermann,

I have some bad news. The answer to your question is yes. Indian men are part mosquito. And the mosquito's constitution starts three inches below the navel. Arguably, Indian men have the

32

poorest leg development in the world. No, seriously, we Indians dare not compare our legs with other races, and it is far safer for us to have other insects such as the Praying Mantis, mosquito, ladybird, and adolescent gnats as comparative studies.

Now obviously, like all bloodthirsty scientists, you'll want reasons. Well, there are many.

We are so obsessed with feet that we are constantly touching and washing and then touching, again, our elders' feet. When we want to show our disapproval, we throw our chappals at what is disturbing us. Chappals, of course, are the dress for the feet. With so much attention given to the feet, it is obvious that the remainder of the leg remains unattended and unnoticed.

India follows the caste system, which is symbolized by the human body. The lower the caste, the lower you are in the human body. You know where that leaves the legs.

However, the most important reason is to do with our shyness. We Indians are inevitably shy and conservative, especially when it comes to our clothing. This is why we are always in long pants or jeans. We are terrified of wearing shorts. Thus, many of us have never actually seen our legs and don't really know about their relative thinness until our wedding night, when we are alerted by the bride's shrieks upon our disrobing. Her shock and amazement and our severe realization leads, of course, to only one thing—early room service.

Now, even those of us who know about our inadequacies deal with it in a very Indian male way, that is, we simply repress it, hoping it will disappear, which in the case of our legs, almost literally happens. Visit any Indian gym or health club, and you'll find tonnes of men working out their upper bodies, while hiding their legs in large track pants.

In fact, which Bollywood hero is famous for his lower body, oh sorry, let me rephrase that: Which Hindi film superstar is famous for his legs?

So, my apologies Ms Jana Pedrowski Chang Boermann. If you want legs, I suggest you move to Taiwan, South Africa, or even Borneo, but not India. In India, we have never heard of them.
Cyrus.

P.S.: All facts and figures are taken from the book 'Pug Aapnee' by the Gujarathi author Srikrishna Saraiya.

34

Half ticket

Dear Cyrus,

Remember when a group of friends go out and attempt to split the bill, there is always the one guy who says, 'Er…guys…I'm a little short'? Well, my boyfriend's that guy. Literally. No, really. My boyfriend is what we politely refer to as a half ticket or in mall terms, a 50 percent off. A shorty. A chottu. A real tingoo.

And since I first started dating him, he seems to have gotten even shorter. We always get stopped at bars where the bouncer frisks him for ID or homework. Things have recently taken a turn for the worse. Recently while crossing a maidan where a game of cricket was in progress, the ball rolled up to me and a 10-year-old boy yelled to my boyfriend, 'Tell your aunty to toss the ball back.'

Please help me with the issue asap! And please don't dare tell me there is no cure for shortness, because the whole world knows that the Chinese have a cure for everything.

Yours truly,

Exasperated girlfriend with a 'minor' issue.

Dear Girlfriend,

Many thanks for your letter. Thanks, thanks, thanks, thanks. I have been shouting about the exact same issue from the rooftops but have not received any official support for it.

Here, once again, we lag behind the West. There, they have accepted the fact that short people are a real nuisance, a hindrance, and a bane. Thus, in western countries, short people have been herded out to the rural areas where they are sometimes mistaken for cattle. To avoid situations like the one you faced in the maidan, short people in Europe are very rarely seen in a public or social gatherings. The last short person seen at a public gathering was Adolf Hitler, and look what that led to. While the West has learnt from their mistakes (the West is now more or less short of short people, except for the Spice Girls and Lady Gaga), we in India continue to take our own sweet time with this malaise.

The majority of the blame in India lies with the shorties themselves. In treating a sickness itself, it's

36

a well known fact that you
sickness. Short people in In
first, that they are, quite fr
Instead, they pretend the
heels, and doing plenty
could be a worse sight tha
high heels and pumps, doing chin-up after chin-up
in a public gathering? Even Hitler didn't resort to
such a complete waste of theatrics.

Unfortunately, just as beauty lies in the eyes
of the beholder, the same goes for short people.
They aren't necessarily the actual sufferers; it's we
'the beholder' who have to take it on the chin every
time we are forced to confront one of these creepy
crawlies. In your special case, you probably dated
him on compassionate grounds—as a favour and
an act of charity and gallantry. Leaving him would
be most unchivalrous and ignoble, although no
doubt extremely tempting. Yet, being a 'little'
guy, he'll need all the support he can get. While
you may be right that the Chinese have all the
answers, you're forgetting they're of little (excuse
the pun) use to either of us as all their instructions
are in Chinese.

However, let's look at a more practical approach
to this…err…smallish problem. The best option is
to slowly wean him away from you. 'Slowly' here

37

e. Please, don't make the same mistake
Gorbachev did when he quite rightly tried
rid of the Soviet Union. Gorby, unfortunately,
nt too quickly for his personal Perestroika.

To be successful, make sure it's a gradual process.
Start first by visiting a park; take a walk by the
children's area. Do this for a few days until a
9-year-old invites him to join the playgroup.
Slowly but surely watch him slip into their world,
and out of yours. Do this at the right pace and
the transition will be smooth. Rush it and you'll be
stuck with Chechnya, Byelorussia, and the Baltic
Republic pulling at your strings. And never ever
forget the maxim, 'the only good short person is a
7-year-old far, far away'.

Chandragupta Maurya had three sons— Samudragupta, Vijayagupta, and Benjamin. Although Samudragupta succeeded him to the throne, the youngest Benjamin (a bit of a maverick), did rule for three days when both the elder boys were having their appendices (plural for appendix in Prakrit) removed. Benjamin at that point, set a very important precedent by walking on his toes. Soon the whole of Magadh and one-third of Taxila followed suit. Now two points are to be noted here. This behaviour cost the Gupta Dynasty their next consecutive seven battles. Secondly, what prompted Benjamin Gupta to act in this way? After all, he was a strapping young lad with all his senses intact, a good education, and three published pamphlets!

Some historians reckoned it was a corn on his right heel which forced this development. However, in 1876 this theory was thrown out of an open window as medical science proved that corns don't occur on heels, especially in mammals. And although Benjamin Gupta was many things, he also most certainly was a mammal. No, my friends, the answer as to why our friend invented the tippy-toe is simple.

Benjamin Gupta was extremely short. To be more precise, he was tiny. No more than four feet seven inches high, and keep in mind that those who dared measure him when he was not tippy-toed were promptly asked to remove their heads from their bodies.

By now, those of you who haven't fallen ill while reading this will say, what's the point of this story?

Let me take that. The point, dear Alice, is this: from that time onwards, men in India realized that a lot of them were actually very short. For sure, tippy-toe worked 2,000 odd years ago, but then there was no Jimmy Choo back then. Today's Indian man, unfortunately or fortunately, has to deal with his shortness in the best way he can—by wearing heels, that is. And let me tell you, when you stand at five feet flat, five feet two can sound very appealing. This height complex has manifested itself in many ways. Benjamin tried to compensate his lack of height by building his muscles. And I'm sure you all know what Hitler did—his compensation was in growing the moustache.

The Indian male has in turn done many strange things. For one, he insisted on only marrying women shorter than himself. As this became increasingly difficult to find, Indian women were instructed to bend permanently so as not to frighten prospective, yet tiny, bridegrooms. Others took to climbing mountains. Some never came down from their trees. Others stayed on ships forever, following the simple level of perspective that the further you are, the less the likelihood of your size being ascertained. This is why opera tenors always stand at the back of the stage, this and the fact that it often takes them half the opera to waddle towards the front.

The short man's complex is also one of the main sources of the Indian male's irritability and crankiness. Let's face it, when is the last time you saw a tall man lose his temper? Have you seen a cricketer walk out of a test match? Sunil Gavaskar? Yes. Not Kapil Dev. Who then, is more likely to lose it in public, Salman Khan or Amitabh Bachchan? India, in her short span of 64 years, has fought four wars and twenty odd skirmishes. Why? Let me assure you the average height of all our prime ministers combined is just 5 feet 4 and a half inches. In the last sixty years how many wars has Norway fought? The answer, in Norwegian, is zero. The combined average height of Norwegian leadership is six feet two and a half inches. Shoe stores specializing in high heel footwear for men were the first to get laid off in Europe's recent recession. India's richest men? That's right, shoe store franchise owners!

41

Demographically, it's amazing to see where the shortness epidemic is at its...err...height. Or to put it more cleverly, in India, where exactly is the height of shortness? The answer may surprise you, but the largest number of short Indians live in the east. The east is the hotbed of shorties. And this has remained true since ancient times. From those three long days that Benjamin Gupta ruled over what presently is Eastern India. Is it any surprise that the British's original name for the East India Company then was Shorty and Son?

Haath ki safai

Hi Cyrus,

I'm Abigail from Sydney, Australia. I've been dating an Indian boy for three years and two of those were consecutive years. Although he's really nice, three things bother me about him:

a) he's always smiling
b) he's always washing his hands
c) he dances with exactly the same dexterity as a table lamp.

Don't get me wrong, I don't expect Rudolf Nureyev, but a constantly smiling piece of furniture on the dance floor whose only form of movement is to exercise his hands every 45 minutes is not someone I want to grow old with. Please tell me if Pankaj's behaviour is to do with his Indianess?

Love,
Abigail.

P.S.: He's also culturally challenged. He insists that 'Tango' is a soft drink. The 'Samba' is a food substance. And Rhamba is a building in South Mumbai.

Hi Abi,

First, let me tell you, I love Sydney. In fact, I had a girlfriend there for many years. Well, sort of. When I finally asked her out on a date, her reply, which still remains imprinted in my brain, was 'I'd rather jump off the Sydney Harbour Bridge.' However, I remained undaunted, and exclusively escorted her inter alia to the Sydney Cricket Ground, and the Sydney Opera House, albeit all in my mind.

But enough about Sydney, let's look at your letter. Okay that's done, now let's turn it around and look at it from another angle. Seems like your problem is to do with one thing and one thing alone—Pankaj. Or to be grammatically correct, Pankajes (Author's note: a collection of Pankajs is called Pankajes). This inability to dance, plus the constant smiling added to the washing of hands is more to do with being Pankaj, than being Indian.

Although I do accept your counter argument, that all Pankajes are Indians, and thus using the transitive property connect, we can conclude that

44

this also, in a smaller sense, is an Indian problem. But while all Pankajes are Indians, all Indians are not necessarily Pankajes, hence for the next paragraph, two sentences, and a drawing, let's stick to flaming only the Pankajes.

First, let us look at the background of our prototype Pankaj. He grew up in New Delhi (any adult who has not been knocked down by a Blue Line bus in Delhi is considered grown up), and went Down Under for higher studies, a sort of paradox in terms. Unfortunately, although he cleared his entrance exams, he hadn't been given a very vital piece of information about Australia. This is the same vital piece of information that caused Captain James Cook to refuse to live in an apartment Down Under. The same reason why, till today, there is no Osho commune in Australia. The same reason why New Zealanders (also known as Kiwis, the All Blacks, or 'those guys'), say they just cannot understand Australia. You see, in Australia they all speak Australian. Pankaj wouldn't have been able to cope. Oh heck, a Pankaj wouldn't have had a bloody chance. He might as well have taken up a job as an aeronautical consultant deep in the Zheng-Xie province of China. This failure to communicate would cause Pankaj to keep a permanent smile

45

on his face as a defense mechanism. All over the world, when a person is in an alien culture that he isn't able to identify with, his response is to smile permanently. President Obama is a case in point.

As for the washing of hands, this is due to another vital piece of information told to all Pankajes when they are little boys, which in India is generally around the age of 22. These boys are told that all Australians are filthy. In fact, all Europeans, North Americans, and Australians are filthy. In fact, the full list is all Europeans, North Americans, Australians, people of the Faire Islands, Coast Timorese, the Kodiak Bear, the Maltese Falcon, the Cyclops, Medusa, her mother, two sisters, and that Bullmastiff 'Gogol'. The poor Pankajes, when trapped abroad, are constantly coming in contact with one or more creatures from this list with the result that they will indulge in constant washing, and if a shower isn't available then the washing will most likely, as it is in your case, be of hands.

Abigail, this sadly is a terrible prejudice and misrepresentation of facts, not to mention a large number of spelling errors.

Pankajes, unfortunately, are forced into believing that the whole lot mentioned in the list are unhygienic. Even though the whole world knows

46

that the East Timorese people as well as the Maltese Falcon, are perfectly hygienic, at least in Northern hemispheric conditions.

About the dancing, all children named Pankaj lack rhythm, just like all children named Pepe ooze rhythm from every pore. There's nothing that can be done really on that score. Yet to save your relationship, you must do the only sensible thing you can do—move to Delhi. In the pristine, curlized, unprejudiced air of Delhi, where homogenous people speak one clear language, Pankaj (to quote William Shakespeare's, Richard the XXIIIrd, Act VI, Scene II), 'may learn to dance *saala*'.

P.S.: By the way, the Tango is a soft drink. The Samba is a food substance. Rhamba is very much a building in South Mumbai which houses the modern miracle of actual parking place.

〰

47

Peter paan

Dear Broacha,

I'm Clare Ryford from the Virgin Islands (No we are not a Richard Branson private limited company, not at least till last Tuesday).

I am about to marry and settle down in India. My husband-to-be is German. His name is Herbert Baer. The name is very appropriate as he has more body hair than the black forest. That is not to say that the black forest is made up of body hair, but you know what I mean.

Now, my husband-to-be has been living in India for the past seven years (actually nine, but in the first two he was in a drug induced state so they don't count). In these seven years he's taken up a lot of Indian habits. The one that he specializes in may actually gain him a ban across Europe. He's addicted to paan. He puts dollops of paan in his mouth, and then when the luger is cocked and ready, he fires in all directions. Among his victims have been our dhobi, our dhobi's son, my visiting mother, our carpenter, the Bhanots (the whole family), Doodles the pug, Sylvester D'Souza and his wife Nishika, a Mercedes Benz car number 2130 (280 set), three taxi drivers, a school principal, and a traffic cop.

The paan stain, once attached to a victim, is almost remorseless and usually cannot be removed, plus there's the added humiliation of being spat on, and in the case of the dhobi's son…it was twice. So, can you recommend a remedy to stop this paan spill before it becomes impossible to return to Europe with him again?

I'm writing to you, not just because I'm desperate, but because I heard you are very cheap.
Clare.

My dearest Clare Ryford,

What an amazing story! A German man named after a large omnivorous predator, who chews paan with a proficiency of an Indian, and spits out the contents in all directions. Amazing! Yes, I'm cheap and yes, I do have a remedy. So my answer to your question is yes and yes and yes, in that order. Now, young lady, while you see some difficulty with this

49

situation, I see opportunity. A great opportunity. I am enclosing the contact numbers of two of my friends. The first is 9819600074, and belongs to my friend who works in a TV channel, which will most likely make a docudrama on your husband and his habits. The Great German poet, his Indian diet and habits will make for some spectacular viewing on Animal Planet. My friend's name is Vinu Garkwad, and I'm sure he'll swallow your story and give you a fair penny for the rights of your animalistic German Indian.

My friend Roshan (whose number is 9910782651) on the other hand, owns a company called Party Planners. They specialize in adult entertainment for adult parties. I can see the German Baer's paan swiveling act becoming quite the rage. A real crowd puller. Personally, I feel a few modifications could make all the difference, like if he comes out of a cake wearing a Roman skirt, nipple rings and with furry hair extensions. This would make the desired initial impact. After which he could kill the audience with his paan routine. I'm so excited, Clare, by the potential in this one that I've created a stage name for your husband—I'd call him Peter Paan, The German Baer, 'Highly influenced by Indian cultural traditions', or maybe, 'Herbert gets your goth'. In

so he didn't have any hair-related implements in his toilet closet. On the other hand, my father had an old school friend called Janak. And Janak was a totally different story. Janak was built exactly like a bull terrier except maybe a bull terrier was taller. Short legs, puffy chest, and a triangular face. When you saw Janak you immediately noticed three things about him:

   a) that he had the longest, richest haul of hair on his head
   b) he constantly drooled saliva from his mouth
   c) his fly was always open.

Janak liked to wear his hair in front of his shoulders in the Hispanic style. This, and the fact that he once drank a tequila shot neat, was his only real connection with Hispanic culture.

Then one day, I witnessed how leading members of the Order of the Comb, conduct themselves, and I must say I was completely in awe. Mid-conversation, Janak stood up to his full height of 61 inches and then reached out to the back right pocket of his jeans. Deftly and in an expert-like fashion the comb came out of the pocket accompanied by a whoosh like sound. The comb was then held by his first three fingers in front of his face, while his left hand cleaned a path in the jungle, his right hand moved down the forest altogether.

53

The two hands worked in perfect harmony in a rhythmic semi-circular motion. But this was not the amazing part. The amazing part was that while executing this graceful move, Janak continued talking all at the same time. Janak employed what veteran comb followers called, the 'rhythm' method. His body would be beautifully balanced—one leg forward, one leg back; then as he swayed back and forth like a man in prayer, somewhere around the Israeli border, his two hands would go to work executing no less and no more than nine semi-circle arcs of his head. The final stroke would be more slow and deliberate. The end would be abrupt and with a flourish he'd hold the pose, right hand with comb over head, left hand parallel to left ear, in much the same way as a bullfighter brandishes his cape at the beginning of a bullfight. Then just as soon as it began, it would end. A flurry of wrists and fingers and the comb would be returned to the back right pocket barely visible to the naked eye (Although I see no sense in the phrase because eyes, as you all know, are almost always naked as a rule).

As I grew up, I noticed many more Janaks lurking everywhere. All had a great common confidence in their art. The only difference was in the treatment—some fought with their follicles, some cajoled and corrected them, and some simply lulled them into a false sense of security in order to manipulate them ultimately. Yet, always, always the comb was returned to the right back pocket once the deed was done.

The Order of the Comb has been around longer than the hills. History is replete with examples of Indian kings who, mid-battle, dropped their swords to return to their combs. Obviously their soldiers followed suit, and the results were disastrous.

The Order of the Comb is unique and found only in our culture, though in Pakistan, Nepal, and eastern Myanmar there does seem to be an underground movement that is constantly getting stronger. Despite its global appeal, the Order of the Comb has remained a more or less Indian phenomenon.

〰

55

Commode-dragon

Dear Uncle,

I'm writing to you because I've heard of your age and wisdom, that too from my carpenter. Yes, that's right, we share a carpenter, and Vishwa Karma tells me that while he fixed your cabinet, you fixed his marriage, and although he can never forgive you for that, he still speaks of your wisdom and vision.

Uncle, recently I married a boy of my parents' choice, and although he's kind to me, and allows me full use of the TV remote, I find his bathroom usage extremely disgusting. Where should I begin? Look, I understand males all over the world forget to put the seat down, but his urine is sprayed all over the rubber pot. I sometimes even find it in the flush. Secondly, he wets the entire bathroom after taking a shower, and he always, always, leaves his wet towel on our bed.

Please help! And, Uncle, how much did you pay Vishwa Karma for your cabinet? I found 30,000 to be a little steep just for fixing our table lamp stand.

Regards,

Madhura Mansabhdhar.

Dear Madhura,

First and foremost, if you call me 'uncle' ever again, I will personally start accompanying your husband in using your bathroom. Wait, not only that, I'll get all my male relatives to join the party as well. And, just for your information, my Uncle Bobby can and does spray it anywhere, which in certain cultures, would be considered a remarkable talent.

Now, let's move on to your problem. To understand this, we must understand our good friend the Indian male a little bit more first. For the Indian male, toilet training, to put it mildly, is mediocre.

At a tender young age, his parents just tell him to point it in any general direction and fire. The inside part of the pot is neither used nor encouraged. Thus, he becomes a sort of a 'freelancer' of the toilet world. He answers to no specific client. At any given time he uses the basin, the shower area, and even that plotted plant that sits by the window (for the more flexible, ahem, members).

As for the pot, he considers this to be his sanctum sanctorum, where he may do as he pleases, or if you'll forgive the pun, as he pees. He decorates this shrine as liberally as he deems fit. As a boy, every time he relieved himself, he would be greeted by a loud cheer from his family and support staff. This caused him to believe, as he grew up, that relieving himself is one of his stronger suits and such an attitude should be seen by the world and not restricted geographically. He may have a bad day at the office, quarrel with his wife, feel low due to the onset of lumbar pain, but when he is alone with his pot, he's a man once again. A gunslinger, who can effortlessly decimate his lethal adversary, who in this case is the...err...um...well the pot.

So, be careful with this situation. To destroy his triumph in the toilet would change a man into a eunuch, and a eunuch is not what you want as your life partner, at least not for the first five years of marriage. Anyway, I have a three-point option plan for you to better this situation:

a) make sure he consumes less liquids. This will mean less visits to the loo and less of a mess for you. This follows of course from Roget's third law of motion that what goes in, must come out

b) if you have the finances, invest in a separate bathroom. The Mughal kings all had separate ones, and you never heard any toilet complaints against, say Akbar

c) grin and bear it for the next twenty years. Then you'll get your revenge. You see, at that point, his peeing will be more of a problem for him than for you.

Yours sincerely,
Cyrus.

P.S.: I've also enclosed my birth certificate, so you can know my true age, or lack of it. I hope this will inspire you to understand that you don't necessarily have to be old to be wise or wise versa.

〜

59

Phlegmbuoyant

Hi,

My name is Masaka Odumbe. I'm a 33-year-old medical student in Pune. Although I am originally from Kenya, I'm told the 'Odumbe' surname is quite common among the ethnic Pune population.

A few months ago while dissecting a cockroach, I fell in love with a boy in my class called Sumit. At first we used to indulge in mundane conversations about cockroach antlers, cockroach legs, and whether cockroaches were capable of expressing emotions such as love, repulsion, and jealousy. Later on it became less about the cockroach and more about us.

We have now been together for one and a half years, but recently the cracks have begun to show. Sumit was never the most hygienic boy but now a few of his habits are really getting extremely annoying. For one, he has a perennial bad throat, so he's always clearing his throat and regurgitating phlegm, which he then swallows with a loud splashing sound. Before starting a sentence, there's always this swallowing spit sound. Of late, this has started getting worse. He's now made the spit module into an accepted Olympic sport. During long drives, balls of spit bounce along across his throat like an old fashioned tennis match involving two equally matched baseline players. He never spits anything out. It's almost like he's started believing in the divinity of his own spit. Now I can't bear spending more than five minutes with him, in fact, I've started missing the cockroaches. Please advice.

Masaka Odumbe,
MBBS.

Dear Dr Masaka,

This time, I must spring to the Indian male's defence. You see, I too suffer from a perennial cold, and this is because the environment that we live in is so unhygienic that it even has the hardy cockroaches dropping like flies. Almost all males (being the weaker gender), carry these colds as proof of their Indianess! This has led to a no-win situation for those who spit out the phlegm and are

61

ostracized for their over reliance on the medieval passtime of spitting in public. Those who are serial regurgitaters are crucified for amplifying the sound that live spit is forced to make while struggling to coexist in our throat.

In a nutshell, due to unhealthy conditions we all get these bad throats, and we are forced to spend hours spitting or regurgitating. Whatever we do, the results are never appreciated by our loved ones.

You'll be surprised, but the health ministry under the guidance of the late Veerappa Moily (he died halfway through his term of suspected tuberculosis, which is the official description given to any VIP who dies due to diseases picked up near or involving the groin region), put up a committee to regulate this whole controversy. They were incidentally known as the Not So Deep Throat committee.

The committee itself consisted of six healthy men, which naturally meant it took nine years to finally formulate. The committee studied the whole business of regurgitation, and found it to be an inevitable conclusion. They reasoned it was part of a 'karmic' cycle that could better be reversed or postponed. Hence the Indian males were stuck with the spit, and the poor females were stuck with the males. The committee came up with some mediocre response to help lessen the auditory agony, such as getting the male to chew substances such as paan or chewing gum, which would merge with the invariable phlegm thus forming a new slightly less obnoxious audio thrill. Also if paan-stained tongues, and paan-riddled open mouths was a far uglier event that a regurgitating throat, or in other words, after some 'paan shock therapy', most people may happily settle for the lesser of the evils.

Dr Masaka, I'm sorry to say you can't run from this situation, and you can't radically alter it. If you decide to stay with Sumit, you will just have to put up with the friends of his who live in his throat. If not, just move on. After all, as the great Kenyan poet M'afuso Bin Jesi put it, 'There are a lot of other cockroaches in the sea.'
Yours sincerely,
Cyrus.

At age eight and three months, I was taken to a very important place in my home city. The place was the northwest corner of the Oval Maidan, the part closed to Eros Theatre.

It was about 6:30 pm, and there were two figures facing the Oval Maidan, standing perfectly still with what seemed to be a torch in their hands. My father asked me to observe them carefully. I soon saw the error of my ways. It wasn't a torch in their hands but something far more sinister. The two gentlemen were indulging in a time honoured Indian-wale practice. A practice that has continued in its pristine form through generations. The art of urinating in public places, without any fear or favour. Okay lets just make that without any fear.

Unlike our Western counterparts, we Indians have never been encouraged to urinate privately in closed secular places (some Eastern Europeans refer to such a place as the 'home'). Our leaders have always pushed for a more public collective display of bathroom etiquette. That is why in India you can happily go up to a man who is urinating on a tree and ask him the time or even directions. He will gladly answer you, and as long as he doesn't resort to using his hands to answer, nothing

64

untoward will come of this exchange. In Europe, if you interrupt someone at a urinal, there's a good chance that the urine flow may be spontaneously redirected…towards you.

Watching the two artists weave their magic on the horribly unhygienic bars of the gates in the maidan boundary, I couldn't help but take in the effortlessness of the occasion. Both the gentlemen seemed to have a very relaxed disposition because of this public outflow.

But who were these men? What type of men preferred public places for relieving themselves, and because of their unusually close proximity, did either man take a sneak peak at the neighbour's canister during the activity, I had wondered?

My questions were soon answered. These two gentlemen were the first two celebrities introduced to me. The third, of course, was the chess champion Bobby Fisher, who was also known to pee in public, and occasionally on the public.

The larger gentleman, who I must say finished his handwork a little quicker, I was told was one of the pillars of Mumbai's business elite. As he shook himself in this vigorous yet regal manner, I couldn't help agreeing that this was the kind of behaviour you'd expect from a genuine multi-millionaire.

65

The other gentleman was very gaunt, and appeared to have eaten only twice in his entire life, and definitely not in the last twelve months.

The two seemed to acknowledge each other's presence and the unfed one passed a scroll with a message to the fed one. The fed one then proceeded to wipe his face with the message and then proceeded to return the scroll to the unfed one, who did the same and then placed it in a back pocket. The unfed one then opened a door of a black sedan for the fed one, and then slipping into the driver's seat himself, drove away.

Distracted by all the goings on, I had momentarily taken my legs of the now golden bars at the Oval Maidan. But what a sight awaited me there! In the same spot where the two champions of public urination had stood, a band of no less than twenty-three people had taken that place. All with the same single objective of adding to the luster and charm, the grandeur and ambience of the Oval Maidan by a little bodily fluid contribution of their own, and that too in the exact same spot where the two pioneers, the Tenzing Norgay and Edmund Hillary of public urination had done their bit for the environment.

My father thus instilled in me five important lessons that day:

a) we all need to pee, publicly, regardless of caste, class, rich, and poor
b) we all like to pee in the same pee zones
c) a good male citizen must arm himself with this geographical knowledge—so he knows where the pee zones are in his city
d) public urination is enjoyed better in a collective; the more the merrier
e) public peepholes are a great place to meet friends and influence people.

🙰

Pet-pooja

Dear Cyrus,

I need some help with my husband. He doesn't seem to be working properly. I don't mean his job, his work life is fine. I mean like a clock that tells the wrong time, he just isn't working properly. Sometimes I do wonder if I would have been better off had I married a clock in the first place?

Where do I start? Okay I'll start here. No, wait I'll start there. No, I think I'll just go back and start there, a place which I previously called here. The moment my husband Ashmit comes home, he lies on his back, assuming the time honoured posture of an upside down frog.

His conversation is limited to grunts. He uses three varieties of grunts. If you ask him if he'd like food, he answers with a single grunt which means 'yes'. If you ask him if he'd like to step out he answers with a double grunt which means 'no'.

If I mention my parents may stop by for dinner, he answers with a number of high pitched grunts, which exactly resemble those made by a man having a heart attack. This conveys his longest message—that he'd be closing his eyes and won't open them until fifteen minutes after my parents have left.

The other day on the dinner table, I tried to initiate a conversation. I asked him if he knew the difference between a rose and a carnation. His reply was, 'Carnations are white coloured dogs with black spots that make excellent firefighters.' And then he promptly fell asleep. His last recorded words that night were, 'pass the chutney'.

I'm only 29 years old! I can't be married to a dead wood for the rest of my life. What should I do?
Yours desperately,
Yasna.

Dear Yasna,

Your problem has everything to do with posture.

All you need is a camera, three shots of vodka and two sticks. First, you need to have the three shots of vodka yourself to make the process less painful. Then take a picture of Ashmit standing in the buff. Pin the photograph onto a wall, and write down what you notice. Not much? 'Correticino senoritaa'. Now look again and observe his posture. You'll find a lump in the middle of Ashmit's (for lack of a letter word) body. That vulgar prolusion is also known as a descended abdomen. This is called a 'gut' by the British, a 'stomach' by the Germans, and a 'container' by the far more pragmatic Japanese (who are known to use it to store undesirables such as stir fried vegetables. Let it be known here that the list of undesirable stir fried vegetables includes all vegetables).

This 'gut', which now looks like a large inflated third knee, is situated in between the two less inflated knees, and condenses 60 percent of Ashmit. As it lowers itself, generally to the tune of that perennial gospel favourite, 'Swing low sweet chariot', it puts an unbelievable amount of pressure on Ashmit's back. Back pain is supposedly the third worst pain you could possibly endure, after death and remarriage, of course. This also explains why someone as famous as the Hunchback of Notre Dame (given name is Kishen), didn't dare marry again because the pressure would have just been too much.

Now we come to the sticks. To help ease his pain you need to do the obvious, that is, inflict

70

some more. Get him to walk around with the stick placed under his arms and behind his back. They will hold up his shoulders, push his chest out, and cause him to have a far better posture. Furthermore, in this position when he tries to lie on his back he will feel unbearable pain, and it will take days for him to extricate himself without external help. Which, by the way, should never be offered. A stick behind the shoulders will limit him severely. He will, for instance, have to rely more on a speaker phone. Visiting the toilet and digging his nose will now become nerve wracking experiences.

This brings us to the second stick, which has a very special function. Every time Ashmit tries to release himself from his new posture, the second stick should come into play. I find three sharp blows to the calf muscle are generally enough. However, feel more than free to experiment with blows on the inner thigh as well. These well-timed and well-administered blows will ultimately only lead to Ashmit's improved posture and future well-being.

Yasna, remember what Noel Coward once said in a dim-lit theatre, 'Spare the rod, and spoil the marriage'.

Yours sincerely,

Cyrus.

71

P.S.: I'm also enclosing a list of people whose posture improved with the two-stick theory:

John Quincy Adams. Kanishka King of the Kushans. The Brothers Karamazov. Akbar. Birbal. The Hound of the Baskervilles. His friend Harry Houdini and Conan the Barbarian, Part II.

N.B.: Harry Houdini's posture improved dramatically but he also drowned as a consequence of being underwater at the time.

Latitudinally challenged

Dear person reading this letter,

I am writing about a breakthrough that I have made. I have managed to figure out a way forward. I think with this information, married couples in India will all have a better chance at happiness, and without the presence of the compulsory omnipresent in-laws. Of course, this information has come at a price. This is my fourth and hopefully final marriage, although I am still only 36 years of age. In all four of my husbands, I noticed the same weaknesses. No backbone, hair in the ears, and refusal to apply soap adequately in their more private areas. In the case of the latter, this caused me to allow the private areas to continue to remain private. However, the biggest problem was the no backbone issue. Initially I thought I was married to amoeba, such was the absolute lack of courage on display. My first husband had the dynamic energy of a dried shell and unfortunately he also had the look and personality of the shell to match.

My second husband was basically comatose. I don't ever remember him actually standing on his feet even once. My third seemed to have regressed to age seven, so while there were signs of life in very fundamental form, the conversation was basic and often was in rhyming verse. Words like 'ding dong, ting tong' were used for the mellifluous dialogue. This is why I swore to myself that I'd raise the bar with the fourth. (By the way, that's exactly where I found him, at the bar, face down.)

Although our initial conversation was one-sided as he had already passed out by then, I was drawn to his supine symmetry, that is, in terms of form.

In sober moments, he displayed some signs of movement and the occasional sign of life. He even joined a yoga class, where he showed signs of improvement even though he was always fast asleep halfway through it.

All Indian married men seemed to have an inherent fear of life itself. Something had to be done. So with husband number four, I decided to change tactics. I decided to create a fear far more fearful than the general fear he had been experiencing all his adult life. I decided to raise the fear 'standard' if you like.

If he thought he had felt fear before, he was sadly mistaken. And where would I find this fear of all fears? The answer was simple—in myself. Overnight I turned into a raging inferno. I lost my temper over all sorts of little things, such as his toothbrush facing the wrong direction. Or if his belt had missed a loop, or if he washed his conditioning shampoo off under the mandatory one minute. At first I yelped at him. Then I started flinging things. Soon I fed off my rage like a maniacal beast. The result? I started becoming violent. For a person born to fear, my husband number four was completely outmatched. Within days I got the desired results.

We'd wake up, and I'd see him immediately cringe with terror. Eye contact was completely wiped out. He'd cower in the shower, waiting for me to leave home. Yet the flipside was that he now couldn't wait to go to work, couldn't wait to meet other people online, he'd rush at every opportunity, social or otherwise, to leave the house. Interaction with others suddenly became his thing. New challenges and novel locations became his best friends. Our personal relationship was kaput, but I liberated him from all other forms of fear. Of course, he'll probably never know how much he

75

owes me, although he does know if he dares thank me, I'll bash his head in. Twice.
Ayesha Morani.

Yes, dear lady, you seem to have hit the nail on the head. Perhaps a little too hard, but who am I to complain when you've got the results? The technique you've used here, though an old one, most certainly bears repeating. After all, as a great statesman may have said, 'What do they have to fear if they have much more to fear instead?'
Love,
Person who has been forced to read this letter.

I was pleasantly surprised when I read a paper published by Martin Hill and James Young on the deficiencies of the Indian male. Before I discuss the paper, a word about the authors. Martin Hill and James Young were born three days apart in the same hospital, St Helena, in Worcestershire. While Martin remembers James from that first week in the hospital, James continues, till today, to occasionally mistake Martin for a sponge.

Both were highly gifted scholars; Martin spoke four languages (Greek, Latin, German, and Bihari) when he was just three. However, since no one in the entire county of Worcestershire spoke any of those languages, he had a very lonely childhood, not in fact having his first conversation till seven months after his sixteenth birthday with a visiting Bavarian salesman.

James, too, was a prodigy in his own right. He excelled at the violin and would have played it professionally if his mother hadn't smashed it on his drunk father's head when he was still a lad of nine and a half.

As teenagers, the two boys roomed with an Indian called Ashok at Cambridge. They were fascinated with this experience mainly on two counts. The first was because Ashok was exceptionally heavy, and the second because

77

Ashok charged them a fee for the room. It was in that musty room in Cambridge, that the two young men started their lifelong study on the Indian male.

Here is their published paper, copies of which are with Random House and others with our local bhelpuri wala:

'Indian men are different. It's not that they are not exactly men, it's just that they tend to slouch a bit. Physically they are of different sizes, yet all of them, without exception, prefer to wear jeans that don't fit.

On the positive side, they can be seen to be caring, sensitive, thoughtful, and concerned. And on the flipside, they are caring, sensitive, thoughtful, and concerned about themselves and nobody else.

The Indian male is not very athletic. One in three can touch the toes, and one in seven can even touch his own toes.

In terms of dress, as mentioned before, they are conservatively shy. Sport pants are barely worn, and as mentioned above, ill-fitting jeans are considered 'de rigueur'.

The Indian male loves washing his hands. In one case study, a subject (Ashok, age 24 years, 5 feet 9 inches, 81 kilos, one eyebrow) used up

43 percent of the entire water supplied to the Cambridge University just on account of washing his hands. He averaged thirty-six trips to the washroom daily. This number doubled on the weekends when the subject subjected himself to a copious amount of alcohol.

When frightened or upset, the Indian male performs a unique gesture. He repeatedly taps his hand to the top of his own head. In any other culture, he would be locked away in a mental institution with immediate effect, but in India, where tapping your own head is not seen as a symptom of chronic madness, he thrives.

The Indian male differs from the European male in one very clear aspect. While European males like to walk around in the buff, in a clear impression of oversized peacocks, the Indian male is not at all comfortable in the nude. So much so that very few Indian females have actually seen an Indian male nude. In one case study (Ashok, age 24 years, 5 feet 9 inches, 81 kilos, one eyebrow), a gentleman from India living with two Europeans never once appeared to shower in their presence in a period of well over three years.

In terms of a psychological profile, the Indian male is dashing, debonair, and detached from material wants. This, of course, is only a figment of his own fertile imagination. In truth, he is vain, boorish, boring, and acquisitive. In fact, his acquisitive nature is stronger than in any other species, male or female, being or not. In one case study (Ashok, age 24 years, 5 feet 9 inches, 81 kilos, one eyebrow), an Indian male had acquired 7,000 CDs, 257 DVDs, 308 comics, 459 pornographic pieces of literature, and sixteen wrist watches in one small room he shared with two Europeans from Worcestershire, England.

The Indian male's strongest quality is that he likes to keep in touch, no matter what. In one case study, an Indian male (Ashok, age 24 years, 5 feet 9 inches, 81 kilos, one eyebrow) repeatedly called, emailed, and wrote to Europeans even sixteen years after they had said their goodbyes. And this was in spite of the fact that the Europeans had never once in that entire period of sixteen years or before, actually replied. The Indian beast is indeed a strange one.'

Now, although Martin got run over by an ice-cream truck about a week ago and James is in an institution for the criminally insane which is a pure vegetarian franchise, I think it's safe for us all to say, they've given all us Indian men some food for thought.

He knows his onions

Dear Cyrus,

Okay, first please understand that I'm writing in even though my toe (second on the right foot when viewed from the left perspective, not foot) is causing me great agony. People may scoff at a toe injury, but I have it on record that a toe injury is in the list of top twenty painful areas of the human body. In fact, it is ranked just below the elbow and shoulder and one above the buttocks. Of course, my toe injury itself is a rather bizarre story. The reason for the damn pain is, in a word, onions.

Last November I got married into a family, which, while they are by and large, nice, decent, and courteous people, are also voracious onion eaters. They devour onions. By the kilo. Individually. It's a crusade against all onions everywhere. A collective, cumulative, and calculated assault on the entire onion population in a bid to perhaps one day actually eradicate the onion and make it extinct. We stay in Vasant Vihar, Delhi, and the onion here is on the endangered species list, along with the Sharmas from Daulatabad, our immediate neighbours. The latter's demise will be caused by congenital heart disease, while the poor onion is going to be exterminated by one family's unbridled passion to consume till death do one of them part.

The effect of this manic, monstrous diet is that I have to stand 16 feet away from any family member who opens his or her mouth. Naturally this is not always possible, so I suffer as a minority struggling to eke out a normal existence in Onionstan.

Three days ago I was exercising on my stepper machine with my iPod on when my mother-in-law pulled out one of my earplugs to give me her usual dose of mundane, redundant, and completely useless information. As a consequence of this, my olfactory senses came within four inches of her onion fragrant filled mouth. Gasping for breath, I toppled over, and while falling off the stepper, I damaged the aforementioned toe. Obviously, for the next two hours, I couldn't feel anything as I was consumed by the awful stale onion stench. My mother-in-law rushed to my side enquiring about my situation in all sincerity, and as a result

of this double whammy, I fainted. Now my worry here is, I do love my husband and occasionally his family too, but how can I get them to give up their biggest, unending, all-consuming passion—the right to devour onions?
Stenched-out Sally.

Onions are here to stay, dear Stenched-out Sally. We can't totally get rid of them. Even Emperor Bindusara and later on two of the Chola greats as well, had sculptures carved of their favourite onions. Though Bindusara's was clearly bigger.

You have entered into a contract with this family already. You should have, at the onset, tackled this deadly problem. Now forcing them to abandon their ways would seem a little too much on your part. I see now that you have three clear options:

a) The obvious solution would be that you too can start eating onions, as this will allow you to be one of them instead of a victim. Remember the saying, 'If you can't beat them, smell like them'

b) You can get to all the supplies, that is, round up all the onion sellers and burn them down. But keep in mind that up to this moment, this may not be allowed by law, and there

83

is a huge possibility that you might find yourself on the darker side of the bars

c) I think the most practical option, however, would be to introduce a substitute, something to slowly replace the good ol' onion. I recommend something similar, something you can cook all foods with, something which itself is like an onion, that is, pungent and uplifting. Garlic immediately springs to mind. It has an even worse smell than the onion. Try to get them to switch to garlic for two weeks. So bad will be the prevalent odour that you yourself will go buy onions as a compromise solution. It's like listening to Madonna and then switching to Lady Gaga, which of course will prompt you to switch back to Madonna again as quickly as possible. And yes, on an unbelievable note, Madonna loves onions.

Love,
Cyrus.

84

Dhoom 4

Paramjit is my name, yaar, but my friend calls me Ducky. This is because of my bad reaction. Yaar, every time I near thee food, I start having these reactions. Now how to tells you, kyunki sharm aati hai, but nevers mind, I will tell. Jab I see thee sarson da saag, certain thing happens. First my friend all walks away. Second, I start becoming thee narvous. And after some time, other reactions happen. Kaise bataun. It is a sounds. A large sounds. We all make these sounds, yaar, but I have not got thee control. Yaar, sach bolun toh it is a sound which doesn't happen from mouth. It is a sound produced at other ends. Now, you understand, yaar. I am feeling the pressure always and my friend they always make thee fun. I make these sounds all different. Ek toh loud bang bang gun kee tarah. Second is like whistle. And another is like blowing the water bubble in the water. Yaar, please mujhe kuch illaj dedo. I'm at wit ends. My friend don't want to hangs out. And hotel and restaurant are asking me to leave. So, yaar, this is common problems only mine is not in proper control.

Paramjit is my name. Ducky.

Duckybhai, yours is a very complex problem, but let me help you out with figures.

One out of five males and one out of nine females have major problems with flatulence. So don't feel ashamed, you actually have lots of friends, or as you prefer to put it, lots of friend.

Flatulence is not very dangerous, the only problem is that it can cause social embarrassment and occasionally lead to a heart attack. The last, of course, is rare. Oh, and remember the person who emits the flatulence doesn't get the heart attack. Instead, an already suffering, highly sensitive and fragile heart patient who is stunned by the sudden explosive sound and corresponding smell, may occasionally succumb to it. Then again, this is very rare. It happened only once in seventeenth century England. Henry VIII let out an extremely large one, which killed off his wife number three, her mother, two Persian cats, a fiddler, and a courier from the court of Spain, who had an undeniable

86

weight problem. Henry VIII, all 390 pounds of him, was, of course, an exceptional proponent of the flatulence missile. It is said that a whole generation of Englishmen gained longer noses because of the time spent pulling at their own.

Yet Paramjit, you amaze me. From the text of your letter, you sound like a perfectly well educated, refined, and cultured man, writing in a foreign language. Surely such a man like yourself will be able to take advantage of all the flatulence control devices available in the market? Gas control pills are a dime a dozen. Now, okay, I understand that just as in the case of condoms, it's embarrassing to ask for a box of GAS EX. Well, simply do what Henry VIII would have done, if he wanted to avoid conversing on this particular topic with his chemist. Enter the chemist shop, find a quiet corner and let out a Paramjit special. You'll be amazed at the speed with which the GAS EX pills will be delivered to you. And if the Paramjit special was truly majestic in volume and appeal, a price may not be charged either. However, if on the slight chance that no normal gas medication is working, please write to me again. I think with the fuel problems we are facing, something proactive can be done with your, let's call it, talent.

One word of advice though. Can you get someone else, one of your friends, perhaps, to write in for you? Consequently you can then proceed to concentrate on holding it in.

Your friend forevers,

Cyrus.

Don break my heart

Dear Cyrus,

Strange as it may sound, I'm married to a man who isn't the man I married. But it's entirely true. When I met Pankaj, he seemed like a really nice young man. Of course, I'm not married to Pankaj. I'm actually married to Dhiraj. Now, when I first met Dhiraj he seemed like a perfectly nice young man as well. There were so many positives about him. For example, he didn't have any major disease. He had a passing interest in personal hygiene, and his was a rare instance of a heterosexual man who wore floral shirts exclusively. In fact, at our first meeting he had a yellow shirt on with large lilac flowers peppered liberally all around. It was the lilacs that were our initial common ground. I just loved them, and he couldn't pronounce them.

Although Dhiraj knew only seven words in English, he used them judiciously enough, and besides I really never had the heart to tell him the preferred pronunciation of 'gorgeous' is with the 'g' sound rather than the 'j' sound, that is 'jorgeous' as he would put it. Dhiraj told me he was in the furniture business and I naively believed him. However, after six months of marriage, I'm beginning to suspect he's a bookie. My suspicion is based on four points:

a) Dhiraj never leaves the house, and he's always on the phone
b) every couple of days or so, suitcases with crores of rupees in cash arrive at our house, and often disappear just as mysteriously
c) his friends call him 'DD'. Dhiraj Dombivali
d) his 'wanted' pictures are posted in every major police station, railway station, and post office.

How can I verify he's really in the furniture business? Please help.
Fiona Patel.

Dear Fiona,

Do I have news for you. First, your husband is in the furniture business. However, he has only one piece of furniture. It's a big block of wood, and he's married to it. You!

90

After reading your letter I asked around, and let me tell you, your husband is among the most famous people in India. Dhiraj Dombivali is better known than the Red Fort or the Qutub Minar. He started his career as a 'fixer' in Dombivali and hence got the tag. Today, he has tentacles that operate from Dombivali to Deutschland. And from Nasik to Nicaragua.

He is so famous that even Polish bookies name their first born after him. That explains why so many teenage girls in Warsaw are called Dombivali. Dhiraj is wanted in thirty-seven countries, and faces the death sentence in four of them. In seven, it's the life sentence. And in nine others he faces much worse—angry wives.

Yes, Dhiraj owes a lot of money in alimony to the nine women he's was married to across the globe. Most of these marriages have come about due to no fault of Dhiraj. Mostly because of language difficulties, misunderstood communication due to certain loss in translation.

He has been using this furniture business excuse since his teens. And it is not altogether false. His father used to supply plastic chairs to weddings but the business collapsed as the comfort levels dipped. They seemed to be more plastic and less chair.

91

The good news, however, is that Dhiraj Dombivali is worth 8,032 crores. The bad news is that nine other wives and the police forces of thirty-seven countries are ahead of you in the line to claim this.

If you still don't believe you're married to a bookie, look out for these four tell-tale signs:

a) the top four buttons on his shirt are always open

b) on his neck and wrist will be at least five kilos of jewellery

c) the last book he ever read had only numbers, not words, in it

d) he carries a shiny gold revolver everywhere he goes.

Fiona, my advice to you is to love him. Your chances of getting a cut of that 8,032 crores are… err…pardon the expression…twenty-six to one. Long odds. If you must date a criminal, date an arsonist, kidnapper, embezzler, even a murderer, as they generally have more stable domestic lives than a bookie. But if you plan to leave him, the next time you date, be wary of anybody in the 'furniture' business, and for God's sake, don't marry someone named after a street!

Cyrus.

Blind faith

Dear friend,

I have been married for a total of nine years, of which I've enjoyed the first four days the most. My husband is a qualified chiropractor, but he doesn't practice as he is not confident of spelling the word in public. Actually speaking, he's a really nice man, and would never have stood out in society except for the fact that he can never stand on both feet; instead, he balances his bulk on just one leg or the other, in the manner of a flamingo. In the last nine years, he's had an assorted number of jobs, including hand modeling, being a mason, blood donor, yogi, and an elephant trainer. He was fired from his last job when it was noticed that his ward Aradhana the elephant also developed this peculiar habit of balancing her entire bulk on just one leg, and when that one leg turned out to be my husband's, you can just imagine the hospital bills!

This brings me to the main problem. Of late he's plunged into a new activity. He's become an art dealer, which would not be such an issue except for the fact that he's colour blind. Now he's gone and invested all our money in four paintings; no, make that three paintings and a sketch. They are—'Nirupama's Nipples' by an artist called Yogesh (the hand of God) Hangal; 'The Bear and the Mountain' by an artist who identifies himself only as 'The White Sleeve'; 'Hitler in Himachal' by Gerald Klung, and 'Seven Ways from Sundown', a sketch of what frankly looks like an old skipping rope by Tomu Cherian. I don't understand art at all and am deeply worried about our investment. Can you please enlighten me on these four works and their value?
Sheepish Shalini.

Dearest Sheepish Shalini,

Fret no more. You are in good hands, that is not vis-à-vis your paintings, but rather vis-à-vis 'MM'.

Whenever I write about art, I like to use as many French words as possible for no apparent reason.

First, congratulations for marrying a man who stands on just one leg. There are many of these available in India presently and thanks for taking one off the market. God knows he wouldn't have had too many takers in any case coming to the art investments. Understand first the difference between an artist and an art dealer. An artist merely paints a canvas. The art dealer has to then convince both the artist and the buyer that the artist's work is indeed a work of art. This he does in four ways:

a) by helping the artist commit suicide

b) by slapping him continuously if he tries again

c) by standing beside the painting and making large orgasmic sounds. (This is more beneficial when someone else is viewing the painting; if he's alone it's probably a waste of time)

d) finally, by repainting the painting—to show him it had obvious colossal flaws—himself. Hence, the art dealer does much more work than the artist, or if you want the easy way out, switch to being the artist.

Yogesh (the Hand of God) Hangal is a rip-off artist. And 'Nirupama's Nipples' is a complete hoax. It's just a poor copy of Rodin's 'The Thinker', albeit with larger breasts. Sell the painting to your local 'raddi' walla and write off your losses. 'The Bear and the Mountain' is a famous lost painting by Nandini Raajkumar, also known as The White Sleeve, simply because she once appeared at one of her own early exhibitions wearing sleeves and nothing else. Clearly influenced by the Ovalists (they followed the Cubists), this painting was valued at three million dollars, sixty-five years ago. However, the painting was lost when Nandini's mother mistook it for a handkerchief and after using it to blow her nose, threw it away in the waste bin. If you have found the original, then you've got a winner. So please, please keep your own mother away from it.

'Hitler in Himachal' traces the possibility that after the Russians invaded Berlin, Hitler became a tour guide and landed with a bus load of tourists in Kashmir, which he found too crowded, so he left the tour there and moved to Himachal, where he spent his last few years as a barber famous for giving a 20 percent discount to people with receding hairlines. Although he tried to keep a low profile, his shop, which was called 'The Fast and the Führer' (Hair Cuts by Adolf Hilter), raked in a good deal of attention. Klung's depiction of Hitler lying on his back with his legs up, imitating a woman giving birth, is probably priceless—if, of course, it's genuine. Klung himself was a former S.S. man, part of the death squad, who moved to India and became an aerobics instructor.

Tomu Cherian doesn't exist. It's a pseudonym used by the Benares con man strangler Pushpa

Kumar Pandey. He's created many 'avataars' of himself to throw the police off his trail. This includes field marshall Valmik, film star Achaanak, soft drink tycoon Parthasarthy Verma, and incubator inventor Shashikant Shivlal Shinde.

An old skipping rope itself will fetch more money than the damn sketch. Keep away from Tomu; he can be very dangerous. As can be Valmik, Achaanak, Verma, and Shinde.

Frankly, two out of the four is not a bad score. I think you and your husband are onto something, so give it a shake. By the way, if the art dealership doesn't work out, then how about you charge the public to view your husband's incredible balancing act? It might just become the next big thing.

Love,

Cyrus.

I've just started breathing again. Not that I stopped breathing altogether. It's just that with the pressure and stress and the pollution generated daily from the Chief Minister's convoy of 370 cars (all unnecessary), my breathing has been affected quite drastically. By day I sound like an adolescent Darth Vader, and by night my voice and breathing, I'm told, is a direct match to Lady Gaga, who despite all reports to the contrary, might just actually be a lady.

Now this breathing conundrum all started early last month when I got a letter from a school stating my daughter's interview was to be later that month. The letter, from what I could tell, was written in the early Egyptian language and had a disclaimer—the interview is not really an interview.

That's akin to being invited to watch a striptease, only to be told later that it's not really a striptease, but instead a 'fully clothed tease'. Although why a house of education would want to put on a striptease or, for that matter, a fully clothed tease, boggles the already fragile mind.

Now, the real problem with the letter, after I had it translated and summarized three times, was the date of the interview which was not really an interview. The date was fixed for November 27, or as I like to call it, two days after my mother's birthday, or as she herself would put it, two days after my father forgot it was my mother's birthday. However, the real problem with the date was that my wife and daughter (who were both required for the interview, which was not an interview) were in America witnessing the birth of my brother-in-law's son. Which, while not quite in the league of the baby Jesus's birth, was in its own small way a rather large event for the immediate family. The letter also stated that my daughter's presence was compulsory, accompanied of course by one parent, or at least a life-size statue of one of the parents, which in Latin cultures is normally also known as the husband.

I immediately consulted an ex-student of the school, who also doubles up as the local oracle; her name is Danish, and from the outset let me tell you, she's not a leg-spinner from Pakistan whose name has recently been linked to match fixing reports. Danish with her positive/supportive personality gave me a sermon of four words: 'You are finished, mate'. (Keep in mind, she had visited Australia in 1986). Her point was that 'no show up, no seat in school'. Danish always likes to talk like a native American to emphasize a point. This is where the breathing altered for the first time.

I desperately called up the airline to prepare the return. However, the airline was closed for renovation. Besides, it was Thanksgiving week—a week where Americans travel the length and breadth of the country giving thanks that they don't have to live with their parents any longer.

As the tickets failed to show up, the oracle tried to boost my self-esteem. 'Better apply to other schools', she assumingly reminded me. My breathing had now been reduced to twice a week. My thoughts had become a deep yellow, hazy sort of colour, and I started fainting with alarming regularity, every fifteen minutes.

Meanwhile my wife, who is the bull to my cow, emailed the school, requesting another date, and wonder of wonders, was granted it!

By now my breathing had almost completely stopped. Forget the interview, which was not an interview, my wife would now return home and blame me for not being able to resolve the issue in our favour. This would be followed by both a tongue and a physical lashing. I wanted to choke the oracle. Unfortunately, Danish was much stronger than me.

But now let's come to the end of the story. My wife and daughter returned. They attended the interview, which was not an interview, and yesterday we got the acceptance letter. Maya will start her new school in April. Oh, wonderful

100

world. Monkey off a father's back. I breathe again. Oh, beautiful, beautiful breath of almost fresh air. At this point I noticed an innocuous white paper attached to the admission form. It was the school fees that had to be paid on admission.

There went my fresh air. And I'm back to not being able to breathe.

N.B. This is actual authentic proof, to show how the Indian male continues to unsuccessfully grapple with the Indian education system. This differs from the Pakistani male who is still trying to find the Pakistani education system, and the English male who can't understand why French is a past of the English education system.

Space—the final frontier

Note: As this letter has been translated from the original Kyrgyzstani with great difficulty, there may be an odd error here and there. Wherever I feel there is an error I've marked a small 'e' beside the word.

Oh Great King, Sultan of the Seven Seas and Lord of the Pickles (e),

Having spent a weekend in your country, I've found it to be smoother than an elephant's tail. A most enjoyable experience for my mother-in-law. Yet I have three questions that I can't seem to find (e) answers to:

a) where exactly is Jharkhand?
b) what is so great about the film *Hum Aapke Hain Kaun?*
c) why do your people always stand so close,

and violate all acceptable norms of proximity in public?

Yours publicly(e),

The Great Wand of Kyrgystan, Naem.

Dear Friend,

First let me say that all Indians are friends of the beautiful country of Kyrgyzstan. Even though none of us know whose it is. Secondly, I hope I've understood your letter, as we really don't have anyone who speaks Kyrgyzstani. In actuality, we used one Tajik chap, along with an Uzbek, and an inner Mongolian guy, who, between them, were able to translate roughly 36 percent of your words.

Then we had to get three other guys to translate, and this whole process kept repeating itself till all our translators left one after another, using lack of communication as their lame excuse. Despite all this let me take a crack at your dilemmas.

Friend, Jharkhand lies in the eastern zone of India, and falls in the East zone's northern part. The East zone's northern part is a stone's throw away from the South zone of India, which lies diametrically west to Jharkhand. Stone throwing, by the way, is still viewed as a recreation in some parts of Jharkhand. Quite frankly, the safest route to landing up in Jharkhand is by getting lost in Bihar.

Now to answer your third question, which you have listed as second. What's so great about the film *Hum Aapke Hai Kaun?* The answer is—nothing.

Finally, let's grapple with your second question, which you have erroneously listed as third. Why do Indians, and Indian men more specifically, violate personal proximity? The reasons for this are manifold but I will list only two or three, as I need to take a nap in fifteen minutes.

The main culprit is noise, and the industrial revolution of course. Nowhere in the civilized world has the industrial revolution had such a profound and ongoing impact as here in good old Bharat. In any of the big cities, be it Lucknow or Ahmedabad, you pop your head out of the window and you'll hear the pleasant sounds of drills, saws, cement motors, tar being filled, hammers, nails, glass being polished, restructured and bridges made, broken down and being made again approximately seven inches from the original site.

These perennial machine-motivated sounds have caused the urban male particularly to lose 75 percent of his hearing. The other 25 percent he loses at home while trying to cope with the hysterical demands of his wife, kids, parents, in-laws, and during the Deepavali festival, the postmen.

Part of this space violation is thus caused because they cannot hear. They are forced to come closer and closer to pick up a conversation and in doing so eventually land up on the speaker's feet, in a direct, but hopelessly helpless case of violation of physical proximity.

Friend, furthermore, there is the logistical explanation, which you must never mistake for the logical explanation. As you probably know external factors like harsh sunlight and music are combining to erode our land in urban areas. Due to these and other mitigating factors such as Members of Parliament deploying more and more cars to transport themselves to any destination that is more than 20 feet away, land in cities is actually decreasing at an alarming rate. However, in the same cities the population of humans continues to go up at an amplifying rate. Conservative estimates say that in the city of Mumbai, sixty thousand Indians are born every day, although on a Sunday this goes down to fifty thousand due to higher hospital charges.

Thus you have a simple equation of less land and more people. When more people are to coexist on less and less land, obviously they'll land up violating each other's personal space. By February 4, 2017, you can expect many Indians to be found standing on one another's feet.

There is another important reason, friend, and this is to do with the average Indian male. Indian men suffer from a fear of being alone. Right from their birth, they are generally the centre of attention, and have no experience of being abandoned or being left completely alone. Thus, at age 22, when they are suddenly exposed to unfamiliar surroundings, they are gripped by uncontrollable fear. This fear causes them to cling to anyone around them, even if the person is a complete stranger with a long beard and a pierced tongue, and with a tattoo of Hitler sunbathing in the South of France on the forehead.

Rather than feel isolated, the average Indian male will stand three inches away from any available stranger's face, sharing the same air, and occasionally making unnecessary physical contact for which he will never apologize. Of course, if the same Indian male takes the stranger to familiar surroundings like his home, physical proximity will no longer be breached and the stranger may be completely ignored. This partly also explains why newly-wed brides, who move

106

in with the groom's family, tend to feel ignored or isolated themselves.

Yours sincerely,

Cyrus.

Yankee-panky

Dear Mrs Broacha,

I've had an unusual experience with India! I loved the crowds and the people. I loved the culture and sometimes counter culture, but am a bit puzzled over the accents.

You see, every time I've spoken to an Indian male, I would receive a reply in a poor rendition of my own accent. The guy speaking would look Indian, appear to be Indian, but would sound like me, albeit, possibly a mildly drunk version of me. Even a one word answer like yes, would be in an accent somewhat similar to my own. My first question here is, was I being mocked by the Indian public because of my accent? Also, I noticed while talking that the Indian male's head would bob up and down at a very fast pace. Again, why do you people have this perpetual nod? Is it some sort of surreal communication that Westerners aren't trained to pick up?

American Tourist (name withheld so you can't mispronounce it).

Dear American Tourist,

First, don't get paranoid. Nobody's mocking you; we're just about the most welcoming people in the entire world. We even have approximately three movies with the word 'welcome' in the title, that is proof if any is needed, of our welcoming nature.

The idea behind copying the foreigner's accent is a very noble one. We just want the guest to feel at home, to feel familiar in our surroundings. By trying to talk like him, we hope we get the foreigner to feel like he's actually with his own people but in much higher temperatures.

Over the years foreign tourists have, of course, reacted differently to all this. For example, Alexander the Great (he wasn't called that back then, he simply went by the monicker Sandy) couldn't handle the various attempts at a Macedonian accent, and ran away in such pain that he actually died on the journey back from India as a consequence. The less sensitive, Timur, about 1,600 years later enjoyed the attempts to sound like him, and hence returned to India to pillage and loot many times in the future. And as a special mark of respect to those who did a good job of imitating his 'Farganeese' (from Fargana) accent, such persons lives were spared, and only their limbs were removed, so as to prevent them becoming a little too over familiar with the Emperor by trying to follow him around.

My personal suggestion to foreigners dealing with these accents is that before coming to India, Armandi rent a DVD of the *The Party* starring Peter Sellers as V. Bakshi, try and copy the accent rendered in the film, and through the length and breadth of India, try and sound like Peter Sellers did in the role of Hrundi V. Bakshi. Your charming companion may then unwittingly sound a little less like you and a little more like his real self, or at the very least like V. Bakshi.

About the head nodding and bobbing, I find I'm doing this even though I'm writing this letter to you, all alone in the secure confines of my closet. This habit, my friend, is in our very DNA. However, this too has what we call, a back story.

Thousands of years ago, as our lands prospered and got more and more populated, we were hit by the problem of less housing and more people. The one person who most greatly suffered because of this was the Indian male. Suddenly, in the confines of his small one bedroom cave overlooking the river where he lived, with his extended family of twenty-two, communication became more and more chaotic. The male would have to answer to, for example, his mother-in-law, his second cousin's step-daughter, his son, and his own maternal grandmother, all at the same time. A few of our ancestors, like the legendary Ravan, could cope with this, as he had, on good authority, ten heads (one shudders at the dentist's bills), however, the average male with one mouth could not handle queries from all these demanding relatives simultaneously. So, our male ancestors started using their heads to answer one relative while the mouth would deal with another. Since 80 percent of the questions posed needed a yes or no answer, the simple hobnob which conveyed both these options became particularly effective. The mouth was saved for answering the wife's perennial question, which is still relevant today, 'Where were you last night?'

Okay and one more thing, although I don't mind being called Mrs Broacha, by calling me this you may cause a whole lot of confusion, as three

111

Mrs Broachas already exist. One of whom may be related to me.
Yours sincerely,
Cyrus.

The North Indian male vale

Cyrus, hi,

I'm known as Sulaxmi from Bangalore. That's probably because my name is Sulaxmi and I'm from Bangalore. I work for a world famous multinational corporation. Unfortunately I'm not allowed to reveal the MNC's name, primarily because my higher ups at General Electric can be very vicious. Since GE is downsizing operations in India, I've been given two options: go to our Delhi branch or just go and never come back, which I am told is one and the same thing.

Now, I'm a little hesitant about shifting to Delhi. Keep in mind I'm a single woman, 31 years old, and am told (by both men and women) that I'm highly attractive (just for your reference, I've enclosed a picture). Can you advise me both on coping with Delhi as well as the Delhi men! Help!

Sulaxmi from Bangalore.

Dear Sulaxmi,

You indeed are extremely attractive, as can be judged by your photograph. Although my wife (who opened the envelope) is still not convinced that a senior executive in a large MNC needs to necessarily distribute topless photography to complete strangers. If you don't mind a little constructive criticism then I'll say just this, the unibrow is no longer in fashion; so two separate eyebrows would be far better appreciated. Also, a pout is a very unnatural expression for most people. Marilyn Monroe could carry it off, Narasimha Rao and a goldfish perhaps, though not simultaneously but for most 31-year-old women, wearing only a pair of socks and a garter, the pout seems a trifle unnecessary.

Sulaxmi, about Delhi—I can only think of the words of the famous Chinese traveller and competitive triple jumper Fa-Hein's reaction. On reaching Delhi he said, 'Wang-tse foor tuk lung.' This roughly translates into, 'Oh hell, can't breathe. Think I've lost a lung.'

First, let's deal with the weather. The Delhi summer is so hot that Muhammad bin Tughlaq had the good sense to ask the whole city to move to a colder climate during the April–May period. Unfortunately, his second choice of Daulatabad, as suggested by his family tour operator Raj Travels, was even worse so the whole city had to immediately return to Delhi. On the other hand, the Delhi winter gets so cold that no Delhite, except for prisoners and politicians (who in any case often double up for one another), dare actually stay in Delhi during the cold season.

In fact, you should only be in Delhi during the latter part of August and the initial rise of September. The exact dates are August 4, 3:15 am to September 9, 4:35 pm. However, as you and I both know, MNCs today are the last of the Banana Republics. This is why GE is listed above both North Korea and Cuba though just under China on the NY Stock Exchange. Such fascist states are going to wipe the floor with you, as that act is clearly part of their manifesto. In fact, that act is actually their complete manifesto. So you had better get used to life in Delhi.

About the Delhi men, here are my words of advice, Sulaxmi—lose the photographs. If Delhi men get a sniff of what they call morally ambiguous behaviour in Punjabi, then the whole city comes to an automatic standstill as all Delhi males (this includes foreign experts and men transferred from outside Delhi), will track you down.

Now, how do you know you're with a predator?

Here's a brief description. Delhi men tend to play with their hair more than other men. They are constantly riffling through or patting down their hair and if they're bald or wearing turbans, they'll switch to tugging at their beards or shirts. Delhi men always stand leaning on one hip. For some reason they feel it gives them a sense of raw power, raging machismo, and animal magnetism. Either that or they just tire easily. Delhi men all wear belts. Though if the belt is sometimes not seen, it is simply because the stomach is covering the belt. The car has to be big, bigger, or biggest. In fact, Mumbai men transferred to Delhi normally get a complex over their colleague's vehicles as they are generally way bigger than their own house was back in Mumbai.

Then the more comfortable a Delhite is with you, the more his rhyming schemes will increase. For example, 'you're looking hot/shot'; 'let's go for a drink/shrink'; or 'check out my car/shar'. And if he really wants to score, he'll say all that at once— 'You're looking hot/shot. Let's go for a drink/shrink. Check out my car/shar.'

Of course, as he gets more inebriated, the rhymes will stop being compatible. 'Let's have another/vanather'; 'do you want to eat/seat?'; 'do you want to sit/tit?'

By all means go on dates with the males available; wine and dine with them, after all you're young, attractive, and single. Only follow my golden rule to avoid unfortunate accidents while out on dates and learn this next part by heart—only go out on LUNCH dates. And don't buy his 'Lets have lunch at night' stuff, their is no such thing.

P.S.: Sulaxmi, if you'd like to take more…err… aesthetically shot photographs of yourself, I've recently invested in a NIKON D35. I'd love to shoot some great photographs of you. Please let me know if you are interested.

117

As an urban Indian male, your life is generally divided into three defining moments.

The first part is life before shaving. Whether one likes it or not, shaving changes a man forever. After all, you are interfering with nature. God or nature or the public limited company that started the world, intended for us to grow facial hair all our lives. This served two clear purposes. First, less and less of the male visage would be exposed as the facial hair would cover up a lot of the facial matter, and remember, advancing age pays havoc with a male's visage. If you don't believe me, just look around you for a bit. Secondly, we could do away with napkins...that is, napkins need not have been invented, as your facial hair, primarily one's beard, would do all the wiping after meals. Shaving thus seems to be an unnatural, needless addition to our lives that has been forced upon us by a group of large bullies, a long, long, time ago, and who unfortunately can't be traced. In fact, research has shown that if you take out shaving and religion from a man's life, you can give him back 55 minutes of his day. Of course, if you take out marriage, you could give him back his whole life. But that's a story for another day. And the sponsor for this chapter, a cola company that can't be named, insists we don't mention marriage at all in this piece or they will withdraw the sponsorship of both the cola bottles they had given us in the first place.

Right, so we've got B.S. (Before Shaving), and P.S. (Post Shaving), and then we have the third defining moment. The club membership interview'. Before shaving you are a boy. Post shaving, you become a man. And after a successful club membership interview, you become a man among other men who also shave. Yet bear in mind there is no guarantee about actually securing the membership, so I have outlined the little process in order that you are armed and ready before daring to face that third defining challenge in your life.

The process begins with a letter from the club announcing that your membership is coming up and you are to meet the committee on such and such a date, and at such and such a time. The letter will compulsorily have usage of words like, apropos, inter alia, and verbatim.

These words must be ignored, as nobody knows what they mean. There will also be an illustration of the clubhouse on the letter. This illustration you must commit to memory, as you may be called upon to illustrate the club at any time by the committee, and this includes after you've been given membership.

Now, please, please respect and observe the dress code. This will, of course, vary from club to club. But one thing is certain, Lycra track pants and pink sequined jackets will not be tolerated. Meat dresses, a la Lady Gaga, will also be frowned upon. Pay particular attention to your shoes. Most of the committee members will be very old. Too old in fact to even raise their heads, and may spend the entire interview just looking at your shoes. So, remember, pay special attention to the shoes.

The interview will take place inside a large room which houses a round table. A pack of twelve committee members will conduct a military-style interview. They will never smile. This doesn't mean you can't smile. Just don't smile too long. Nothing is more awkward than a lingering smile that just receives a harsh glare in return. Don't lean back, that kind of body language you can use only once you have been inducted into the committee. Don't sit too far forward either with your face on your hands. Over eagerness is despised even more than arrogance and over confidence. When a question is asked of you, don't repeat the question.

For example, one standard question these days is, 'Are you or have you, at any point, been a card carrying member of a terrorist organization?' To this your response must not be, 'Am I or have I ever been a card carrying member of a terrorist organization?' If indeed, this is your response then your chances of joining a terrorist organization far outweigh your chances of joining the club. Most clubs have a keen interest in sports. Sports that will win you brownie points include cricket, football, rugby, hockey, badminton, tennis, and swimming. Sports that are not sure shot winners include synchronized swimming, Bharat Natyam, skipping rope, lungri, catching cook, and statue.

While asking questions, members may ask you diverse questions simultaneously. Don't be perturbed, take your time and answer every single one. To loaded questions like 'Are you a practicing homosexual?', always tread on the side of caution. Remember, that an interview is no place for honesty to rear its boring head.

At the end of the interview, thank all the stalwarts and walk out with your head held high. However, take care not to walk out cheering, arms akimbo, like you have just won the Wimbledon, because as everybody knows, no member of your club could ever win the Wimbledon.

If you've walked the middle path, in about a week, you'll get a letter telling you whether you are in or out. Ignore, once again, words like Apropos, Agendum, Habeas Corpus and *Les Misérables*. Instead, focus on one of two words— accepted or rejected.

One of them means your membership has been accepted, although...err...I'm not sure which one.

O lord! The landlord

Dear Cyrus,

My name is Mohit Acharya, and I own a dilapidated building in Central Mumbai. I have diligently followed my grandfather's order of never repairing or modernizing it. His exact words to me were, 'To be successful, keep the rents up and the repairs down.' When a tenant complains about something, I simply provide the same solution—wallpaper. For example, if he asks me to repair a pipe in the bathroom, my response is to cover the pipe with wallpaper. If he says his window has a crack, I provide wallpaper. If he feels a beam is about to fall and wreck the entire building, I give just one and only one alternative, wallpaper.

Yet recently, I've encountered my match. A young boy called Mayank from Jamshedpur has rented the one-bedroom studio apartment on the third floor. The first one month was fine and I greeted all his

issues with my successful wallpaper argument. Three and a half months later I'm told that there are about twenty-seven occupants presently in the flat. When I objected to the numbers, Mayank told me not to worry but instead to send him some wallpaper.
Desperately seeking help,
Mohit Acharya.

Dear Mohit,

Let me begin by saying your name four times—Mohit, Mohit, Mohit, Mohit...sorry, five times even, Mohit. What you're facing is hardly a unique problem. We Indians are famous for being twenty to a room. As a landlord, you should have braced yourself for it; it was bound to happen.

Obviously, you don't want to go to the authorities about this over occupancy business or your little wallpaper trick may be exposed. Stopping water and electricity will have no effect keeping in mind that out of twenty-seven occupants, more than half would have no access to electricity and water amenities anyway.

You have three options that you could try, but none of them will actually guarantee you success:

    a) you may introduce a female guest. This may cause a spirit of competition and infighting among the occupants, but this may also have a reverse effect, as one or more tenants may breed with the new guest, which will result in more tenants. Just that these new ones will be shorter, smellier, and far more demanding

b) you may offer Mayank a large sum of money to move out. However, while Mayank may very well move out, the remaining twenty-six may very well stay put, and more importantly, replace Mohit in a heartbeat

c) you may sell the building as quickly as possible. This may probably be your best option, as you will keep your promise to your grandfather and maybe use the money to start a wallpaper business, which in any case seems to be your life's real passion.

Unfortunately, social studies have shown quite irrevocably, that when we Indians move into a place, we multiply faster than any other nationality or species or plant or animal. Just take a look at what we've done in England or Canada as an example.

Don't lose sleep over this as there is a good chance that authorities will tear down your dilapidated building in the next five years. Then the tenants will be their problem.

Cyrus.

125

Needy Gonzales

Hi,

My name is Apurva Mahadik. I'm studying in the twelfth standard for the first time. My problem is that I don't have any friends. Even the chowkidar who I wave at every morning has stopped responding. Now whenever I wave at him he pretends to have a seizure by holding his chest and coughing violently. He then covers his face with a handkerchief until I've left the scene.

My mother says this is because of my acne, my father says it's my halitosis, which was a gift from my maternal grandfather along with baldness, weak-knees, and chronic indigestion. Of course, my paternal grandfather was far kinder—he left me ten shares of Bajaj Auto, an unmovable Ambassador car, a damaged liver, asthma, deafness in the right ear, and worst of all, four pictures of him in the shower, taken in a seductive manner, when he was of the age of 86 and seven months.

Why can't I have friends? What must I do to lure people? Do you think the chowkidar has genuine health defects or is he just trying to avoid me? And will you be my friend?
Apurva.

Dear Apurva,

First and foremost, let me reassure you that the chowkidar is 150, no 200, nay 1,736 percent definitely trying to avoid you. The exact reason is difficult to pinpoint. As someone in the unwanted business, you have got some serious potential. Whether it's the asthma or bad breath, you have got an entire gamut, the Grand Slam, the jackpot of authentic reasons to be seriously avoided. In fact, let me level with you here. After reading your letter, I immediately went down for a wash. Seven times. With Dettol. I've also wrapped your letter in a thin polythene bag in order to sanitize it and I also plan to burn it immediately after I fax my reply, from someone else's fax machine.

Now let us turn to the great analyst Carl Jung's brother Paul, who had the good sense to persevere with his chosen trade of singer/songwriter. It was Paul Jung who suggested (shortly after his ninth marriage collapsed along with the bridge on which the couple was taking their vows), that people are avoided by other people for the following reasons:

a) because they are wet
b) because they have abrasions
c) because they are communists
d) because, in spite of the fact that they are wet, they continue to behave like communists.

If none of these reasons make sense to you, then we must turn to Paul Jung's younger brother or if you like, Carl Jung's older brother Kim who in his book *Alone Again* pointed out the reason why people avoided him—the most crucial reason being that he was 'needy'. Kim should know, as neither of his brothers spoke to him for thirty-seven years, and then they did it was only because of the invention of the telephone. Which obviously allowed for communication without any contact, visual, or otherwise.

Apurva, yours is the classic case of a person who is too needy. Nobody likes a person who always says hi, always says bye, always wants to have a kind word, always wants to share a reassuring smile. The fast-paced, cut-throat, dog-eat-dog modern world has no place for needy people, also known as the 'needy'.

Have you noticed that even in your building, while you slow down to engage an oncoming person in dialogue, the oncoming person in turn

128

keeps his head down, avoids eye contact, quickens his pace, and shoots right past you? Well, this is a natural reaction to needy people by a normal person. As a child, did you send out three invites per child for your birthday parties? Plus seven to eight reminders per day? Do you even wonder why the other boys insisted you stand next to the balloons at the air-pistol shooting range at the local fun fare? Do you really think it was so that the nailed-in balloons wouldn't fly away?

Apurva, as a needy person you have suffered rejection and avoidance all your life. A person like you must be treated in the most sensitive and delicate manner. To answer your question about whether I'll be your friend, may I, without a moment's hesitation say, 'Of course not'. Never in your wildest dreams. I'm choc-a-bloc filled with friends right now, and besides a needy person is like a pollutant. Allow one in, and the rest of the group will avoid you as well.

I suggest you carry a cap, a box of mints, and a breathing pump and for God's sake leave the poor chowkidar alone. And never forget Kim Jung's dying words, 'A vice may well be a vice, but it's far better to be greedy than needy.'

Warmly,

Cyrus.

P.S.: Please stop e-mailing me. You have already contributed to the most boring chapter in the book. I can't possibly correspond with you again.

My Christmas may be celebrated with a cow. And I don't mean in the same way some people celebrate Christmas with a turkey. Although in this particular case, a turkey may be an easier option.

The whole thing started a few days ago. I went out to have a drink with a friend. I did have a drink, but I had a drink many times over. The result was the slowing down of all the senses, especially the one that is rarely used in marriage—the memory. What I do remember is that approximately around 'a' drink No. 7, my friend introduced me to a friend who, according to 'a' drink No. 8, was quite delicious. Now the problem with delicious women (and here it matters little whether you're drunk or sober) is that, according to Einstein's theory of relative beauty, 'in the presence of a woman who is delicious, a man's reaction will always be the same, that is, he will want to please her'. On this same occasion I found, sadly, that I too, at the end of it all, was an ordinary man. The woman was speaking about her love for animals. My response, aided by 'a' drink No. 9, was to bark like a Doberman Pinscher. Sorry, make that a Lhasa Apso. She, I think, mentioned something about a sick cow that needed a home. I think at this point I stopped barking. Then 'a' drink No. 10 asked me to make a cow sound and I couldn't for the life of me remember what sound cows make.

The delicious woman went on about the spirit of Christmas and the art of giving. I responded in the most sincere form possible. I vaguely said (and remember, by 'a' drink No. 11 even Attila and Alexander didn't know which country they were in) that it would be a badge of honour for me to give this sick bovine a house, as a Christmas message to not just her but all cows. The delicious woman kissed me on the cheek, then noted my phone number and promised me delivery of the cow on Christmas. As 'a' drink No. 12 dissolved safely in my stomach, I remember inquiring if she had any badgers, falcons, water buffaloes, and mountain gorillas, all of whom were welcome to celebrate Christmas with me.

The next day I spoke to my friend, hoping that none of it ever happened, no delicious woman and no bovine that is. Mind you, I was already a little shattered that the friend existed in the first place. Doubly shattered when he confirmed the story of the cow. Now came the real issue. How to break the story to my wife? My wife's not really into the whole 'spirit of Christmas' thing, and moreover, any story that I've previously told her which has begun with the words 'I met a delicious woman...' has always ended a little badly.

But with only 48 hours to go before the delivery of the cow at my doorstep, I had to tell my wife something. I had four options:

a) I could join the Salvation Army
b) shave my facial hair and pretend to be her sister
c) move residence, so that I'm not there when the cow checks in
d) Reason with the cow.

N.B. The story has been included for no other reason but the noble one of animal awareness. Since the average Indian male and the average Indian bovine are both categorized under the above classification, the story must stand.

133

Aap aise queue ho?

Dear Sir,

I hope this finds you well because, quite frankly, that makes just one of us.

My name is Igor Rassovich and I'm an exchange student from Byelorussia. Although I've enjoyed myself in India, I still can't understand the behaviour of Indians in an airport check-in queue. The other day I was the third person in the queue, yet I missed my flight as the first two customers took over 40 minutes to check-in. The first passenger went through each and every seat preference, and then spent over 10 minutes fighting over his four check-in bags, which were tweny-nine kilos above the weight limit, as was his wife and both his children.

The second guy wanted all his frequent flight miles added from his previous ninety-seven flights, and then proceeded to give his wife a running commentary of his present status over the phone. 'Yah, I'm presently about to check-in. They say the plane is on time but I haven't seen the plane, and I can't say for sure. No, I forgot to take my multivitamin in the morning but I'll take it on the plane if the flight's delayed. Though I can't say because they say it's on time, but I haven't really seen any plane so far, did Sharma call, dear?'

Why do you Indians waste so much time in check-in queues? Why can't you just get to the point and move on? Thank God, Rome wasn't built by Indians. Forget a day, imagine how long it would have taken if there was an Indian contractor in charge of the project? And for God's sake, who the hell is Sharma?

Igor,

F.F.O.I. (Former Friend of India).

Dear Igor,

Don't be an ignoramus. Stop grumbling like a complete imbecile. As opposed to a partial imbecile which is a far less severe state of mind.

You foreigners come over here, eat our curry, drink our wines, which very often are your wines that we smuggled in the first place, bed our women, and then have the audacity to complain about all things Indian. If I had a frequent flyer mile for

135

every foreigner's complaint, I'd have overtaken Neil Bloody Armstrong by now.

First, the food. Then the water, then the crowds, the dust, the diseases. And now the check-in at airports? What's the big deal? Yes, we are a slow people but it's clearly not our fault. I'll let you in on a secret—it's in our genes. We are the only species (along with perhaps the flamingoes, which stand on one leg contemplating long and hard whether to switch over to the other leg) who have a procrastinating gene. That is, the gene itself doesn't procrastinate, but it does cause us to procrastinate. To be honest, I'd have finished your letter two days ago when it first came to me but after opening it, I picked up my pen, wrote your name down, 'Dear Igor', and then procrastinated. I can't specifically tell you the details of my procrastination exactly, suffice to say, that like the flamingo, I seemed to have at least one leg off the ground all through that time.

We Indians are proud of our procrastination. When Alexander crossed the Indus and marched towards King Porus, the battle was scheduled for 4:30 pm. While the Macedonian and his party of four reached the site three minutes early, Porus was, well nowhere to be found. Porus finally sent a message to push the battle to Wednesday, as he was still at lunch. It's another matter that Wednesday was no good for Alexander as he was aiming to get a hair cut on that day, and another matter that Indians and Jesuits don't do battle on Thursday and Porus suggested Friday, which was the Greek weekend. Show me one Greek who works on his weekend and I'll show you a flamingo on two feet simultaneously.

Due to a mixture of Porus' proclivity to procrastinate and Alexander's billion Greek, Macedonian, Persian, and Mede festivals, the battle took five years and seven months to commence, even though throughout this entire period Porus and Alexander were not more than thirty feet apart, and kept exchanging notes on hair care. My point is, yes, we take our time in queues. Yes, we can jam an airport check-in counter with just two slow and deliberate passengers, putting up an Olympic standard show in procrastination manoeuvres. Yes, we ask more questions, carry more bags, constantly change our minds, and resort to mobile phone breaks, but I repeat, it's not our fault.

Just like a Scotsman can't be blamed for having red hair.

However, unlike other countries, we have been magnanimous enough to protect our foreign tourists from becoming mute victims of procrastination.

Haven't you heard of tele check-ins? That's our way of safeguarding you from our uncontrollable urge, our insatiable involuntary need, our primal and foremost instinct to stand on one leg and imitate a flamingo.

Yours, ever so slowly,

Cyrus.

138

Foreign exchange

Dear Cyrus,

What a wonderful country India is. Really, I've had the most beautiful experience, life-changing, soul-altering, far-reaching, and more. I came to India from Sweden with four bags. I leave India with just a cup and a whole lot of memories.

I reached Mumbai airport from Gastaad (please don't do any rhyming jokes) two months ago. I immediately found everyone to be very helpful, and all around me Indians seemed to be smiling. Outside the airport I met a good Samaritan called Vinay, who offered me a seat in his taxi. For a meager sum of five hundred dollars (Rs 22,000), this soul agreed to drop me all the way to the Leela Hotel. A distance of at least half a kilometre. Throughout the four-minute ride, he explained the rudimentaries of life in India. Since he spoke in Hindi, I of course didn't understand a word. He even offered to come up to my room and give me a full body massage for an additional 1,000 dollars, but since I held an already crowded agenda, I had to politely decline.

As I checked into the hotel, I noticed that one of my four bags hadn't actually made it out of the taxi. I couldn't help feeling bad for Vinay, who'd probably spend the rest of the day trying to get the bag back to me. Mumbai was great. I saw all the sights, the Gateway of India, the Asiatic library, Shri Sharad Pawar, etc. I also got to see something very rare. How the whole city came to a standstill to allow the busy chief minister to go home. The chief minister does so with the help of 107 accompanying vehicles. Only the very richest states in the world can actually bear witness to such a feat.

From Mumbai I went to Jaipur. Here for just 2,000 dollars (Rs 1 lakh), the camel wala let me ride his camel for a whole three minutes, which I used to good effect on another camel wala who was getting very agitated that I didn't ride his camel in the first place. From Jaipur I crossed to Benares, where for just 5,000 dollars (Rs 2.5 lakh), I was given a bath in the Ganges. (Of course, they charged extra for cleaning the privates and extra for using soap).

Now, didn't want to seem like a super-wealthy vulgar European, so I restrained myself. After this, I visited some famous temples where I gave a voluntary donation of just 10,000 dollars (Rs 5 lakh). However, the townspeople had the good sense not to scoff at my pitiable act of charity and insisted on treating me as one of their own. This I soon realized when they insisted on keeping one of my bags as a momento to remember me by. They even charged me half rate for the usage of a towel, just 20 dollars (Rs 1,000). These are the memories that I will cherish the most. From the Leela to the airport I got a free transfer from the hotel. The driver assigned to me was a splendid fellow called Akhil. Akhil told me of his mother who needed a heart by-pass, an operation he could ill afford. He seemed very content with my offer of my last 10,000 dollars, my Rolex watch, and both my last pieces of baggage. This proud and noble warrior then insisted I give him my Swedish address so he could repay the money in two weeks' time.

As I boarded the plane to go back home, I couldn't help but wish that we Europeans would one day be as giving, charitable, and open as my Indian brethren. Thank you, India.
Lasse Gallestsomin.

Well, Lasse, what can I say, life and experience is what we make of it. You seem to have got a heck of a lot out of your trip to—the mother of all countries—but whether India got anything out of you is a matter open to debate. Lastly, suffice you to think India was a gracious host. Here's a small suggestion: why don't you give Pakistan a visit next time around? You may find the visit strikingly similar.

Cyrus.

No guide to India and the Indian male would be complete without mentioning one of India's favourite and dominant communities, also known as the poor.

Well before the Aryan invasion, well before Dravidian dominance, well before whatever was well before that, we've had them around—the poor, that is. In other times, tourist guides will always have to be forced to refer to them. They would say, 'Ladies and gentleman, on the left is Hotel Varanasi, on the right the holy Ganges, and between them the poor. Please take in the first and second sights as we will soon run out of them, unlike the poor, who we will find in surplus and generally in mint condition all across the heritage sights.'

India has always had the poor. However, even Indians are unaware that the poor fall in two categories. Those who are really poor, and those who pretend to be poor. The really poor consist of farmers, villagers, circus performers, and members of the party in the Opposition.

Those who pretend to be poor include beggars, bureaucrats, retired cricketers, life-long lifters, bar dancers, teachers, and servicemen. Now, we cannot analyse all these sub-groups in just a couple of pages and that too free of cost! So let's look at a segment in this sub-group, the common beggar.

143

The common beggar works in shifts. His office is between two traffic signals. He earns anything between Rs 30 to Rs 30,000 per day. His first rule is, he never gives a cent to charity. He doesn't pay any tax. He doesn't pay any rent. He has no overheads, no expense on electricity, gas, water, or mobile phone. He usually avoids keeping a car so doesn't incur any costs on petrol, or driver and his overtime.

He never goes on holiday. He doesn't pay his work force. He has not yet invested in a fixed office address. He avoids club memberships. He doesn't waste time and money on hygiene products. He keeps nothing in the way of personal consumption. He has no clothes, no deodorants, no bracelets, and no shoes. He's not one for dining at fancy restaurants, unless he gets good service on already paid for food outside the establishment. He's not majorly into electronic goods, and if he does own a hand-me-down computer, he'll make sure it comes without a printer.

Beggars in India are among the most privileged. Since they work in the outdoors, they work in short shifts, and rotate their services. Since they pay no tax and have no overheads, and, in fact, don't really exist on paper, they are the only professional who make a 100 percent profit on their earning. The only professionals. Although a couple of politicians may like to argue that point a little further.

There is one drawback though that has been noticed in this super successful beggar community. Along with success, some amount of cockiness and overconfidence spills into the community. Especially among the males, who, drunk with an over extended idea of their self-worth, tend to do what males all over the world tend to do when under the influence of success. That is, they copulate. And as the old Tibetan poem points out, 'Copulation leads to population'.

And you don't need Ramanath to tell you that success, when divided among more people, means less success per person. So in a sense, their success is now threatening their...err...success. With the market share dipping, beggars may, in the coming generation, have to look unthinkably at alternate means of income. Inevitable as it may sound, the beggar community may have to go against the very fundamental principle that levels them universally. Go against their very own calling card, their mantra. Yup, unthinkable as it may seem, the day seems not so distant when beggars may, indeed, be forced to be choosers.

In fact, in the next thirty years or so, India may see less of the sights that we take for granted

145

today, that make us uniquely Indian. Sights such as the Irani restaurant, the paan stain, the ill fitting trouser, the wrongly spelt roadsign, the pigeon droppings, and that proud professional, the Indian beggar, While we cry ourselves hoarse to save the tiger, or the snow leopard, lets not lose sight of the beggar. Lets hope the beggar doesn't go the way of that damn bastard. That poor damned great Indian bastard.

The sum of all Indian marriages

Dear Person,

I'm a third generation American of Indian descent. Recently my parents divorced after thirty-three years of marriage. I was aghast. I was even more aghast when my American friends told me that in Indian culture, parents are not allowed to divorce each other without first getting their children's permission. Somehow I feel the whole mess is my fault as I had failed to assert myself in time to stop this partition. Also, I feel I don't understand my parents, my culture, or my roots. Confused Desi Chris Trisnama.

Dear Chris,

Before dwelling on anything, let's first understand who the average Indian male is vis-à-vis the average Indian female. To get you to understand 'our' language better, let's call it the average Indian phemale!

The average Indian male today is (and we're talking very average here) small, large, small. While this may sound like an order at whiskey bar, it generally isn't. You see, the average Indian male is small from his neck upwards, largish between the neck and legs, and small again in the lower floors of the building. This doesn't quite match the average Indian 'phemale' who follows the small, small, large design.

Now let's talk mathematics and especially equations. Small + large + small $\neq$ small + small + large. Except for neck upwards where we are both small, it is actually quite a mismatch. In purely mathematical terms, the Indian male + female has 33.3 percent going for it and 66.6 percent against.

Contrast this with a Caucasian couple where the male is larger + larger + larger = the woman who is also large + large + large. Hence a perfect fit.

Due to this data now being available, we realize that an average Indian couple in a relationship is actually up against each other. This also explains why same sex couples are seeing larger and more fulfilling relationships in our culture today. Now,

148

although 66.6 percent of our equity is incompatible, this problem is not insurmountable. Just as a person with poor eyesight offsets this disadvantage through the use of glasses, or an Indian politician offsets his lack of crime, by accepting brown envelopes, an Indian couple too can offset their imbalances by following a few basic rules:

a) never remove clothes in front of one another; if you're forced to do so make sure you've got another pair of clothes underneath your original pair. This also obviously means you can't go swimming, or to the beach, skinny-dipping, or shopping together either!

b) stick to the telephone, as our compatibility is in neck upwards relationships based on phones and e-mails, well, rocks. Research has shown that the best relationships between Indian couples are those couples who for years have communicated through phones, letters, and e-mails and who have never actually met. Play to your strengths; keep the relationship restricted to phones and the like

c) get the relatives out of the picture. Relatives too play too large a role in Indian relationships. You are well advised to keep their role to a minimum from the beginning.

149

This is done in two ways: a) ignoring your relatives and b) denying you ever had a relative.

Chris, your parents can still get back together if they follow these three simple rules: a) they must remove all traces of relatives from their lives b) they must never swim together again c) they must restrict their relationship to emails or phone calls. Pictures may be exchanged but not much else.

And remember this Golden rule above all else—if they are to get back together, then to enjoy a fruitful and evolved second innings, under no circumstances, and I cannot stress this enough, under no circumstances are they to actually ever meet.

Then, and only then will small + large + small be in harmony with small + small + large.

Yours sincerely,

Cyrus.

Jungle mein mangal

Dear Dr Broacha,

I am sleepy in Jalandhar. I got married about six months ago. At the moment, my husband is in Bangkok with a couple of his male colleagues. He said he wanted to experience the wildlife in Bangkok. I found this a bit peculiar because in the last six months he hasn't really shown any inclination towards wildlife whatsoever. He has never ever mentioned a dog, looked at a cat, or even bothered to pat a plant. The closest he came to experiencing any wildlife is when he tried killing a mosquito unsuccessfully and thereby fractured his finger on our dressing room mirror.

Now, around the same time that he left for his wildlife safari, I started seeing dreams for the first time.

My first dream began with a tall man trying unsuccessfully to enter a room though a key hole.

After forty-three such failed attempts, he then tried to eat the key hole. At this point, a giant tidal wave rushed toward him. Then, suddenly and surreptitiously, the tidal wave slipped into the key hole and disappeared into the house, all the while laughing uproariously in the tall man's face.

In my second dream, two female gorillas were fighting over a man, that is, they were not fighting over his love; in fact, they were fighting over who gets to eat him. The man himself didn't seem to particularly care who eats him as long as they didn't start devouring him head first.

In the third and last dream, ice-creams had taken over the world. The entire world was colonized by ice-creams. Ice-creams of different flavours (and both cone and cup varieties) controlled nuclear weapons, power plants, medicare, water, gas, electricity as well as all state-run swimming pools and floatation devices. Sports bodies, entertainment, off-Broadway plays also fell into their purview. It was an ice-cream raj in a true sense.

Doctor, I cannot interpret these dreams. I mean, are they Freudian in nature with Adler-like undertones, or are they more Jungian in body with shades of Maslow? I can't quite tell.
Sleepy from Jalandhar.

152

Dear Sleepy,

May I begin by saying I no longer use the title doctor, although I have retained my other titles such as Il Duce, Pele, and La Sombrero.

Dreams are a fascinating subject. The interpretation of dreams, however, can be severely dangerous. Napoleon Bonaparte went on a world domination trip because he dreamt that he was one inch taller than he actually was in real life. Muhammad Bin Tughlaq moved the capital from Delhi to Daulatabad because he couldn't quite interpret his own dream. You see, his dreams were in Turkish, and he spoke only Persian; this led to great confusion. In your case, let's try and analyse and hope we get it right.

In your first dream, where a man is trying to pass through a key hole and then is psyched out by a tidal wave that does the same with immaculate ease, this is commonly known as the Pavarotti personification. Here, people who consider themselves overweight suffer from lower and lower body self-esteem as many fitter and healthier people continuously pass them by.

But why anybody would want to pass through a key hole is beyond the realm of science and is best answered by a heavy dose of substance abuse.

153

Your gorilla dream has me particularly perplexed. The gorilla is largely vegetarian. The female gorilla, always careful about her figure, is even more so. This dream would make much more sense if two women were fighting over a gorilla instead. Let's face it, the chances of a woman eating a male gorilla are much higher than those of a female gorilla eating a homo sapien.

Your third dream is the most clear of all. Ice-cream domination is a very common theme, and not just to ice-creams. An ice-cream represents something pleasurable, and when something pleasurable is running things, it makes you happy. In short, you need much more pleasure in your life.

These dreams are probably Freudian with no trace of Adler or of Jung, but definitely with a hint of Maslow and possibly the artist formerly known as Prince.

Sleepy, a word of advice about your husband. There is no wildlife in Bangkok. Thailand perhaps, but not in Bangkok per se. Indians go to Bangkok for one thing and one thing alone. So don't be naïve; your husband has gone to Bangkok for one thing, and that is to stitch suits. Confront him about it, and ask him to make a couple of suits for you too.

Anyway, all the best and happy dreaming.
El Sombrero, alias El Paso, alias the Black Swan,
alias Sheila, alias Pele, alias II Duce, alias Deepak
C. Chopra.

Very few things worldwide have caused as much trouble. You can keep your communal polities, diversity in incomes and class, proliferation of weapons, both conventional and otherwise, you can keep your ethnic cleansing and racial nullification horror stories. None of these will cut it with me. I know the truth. This truth cannot lay covered in secret any longer. More human conflict and anger is caused by…well, how do I put this… err…by the average Indian male's driving skills. Yes, driving. In Latin it's known as sitting behind the wheel of a vehicle.

Let us look at this sinister phenomenon in a methodical and scientific manner. Human conflict worldwide is caused because of the temperamental, and henceforth, operational diversity between three broad groups of automobile enforcers, who can also be called by their salaried version—drivers.

Temperament one is the 'speedy Gonzales' type characterized by illustrious names such as Nelson Piquet, Juan Fangio, Michael Schumacher, also my mother. That is not to say that Michael Schumacher is my mother. That would be far, far from the truth. Yet to put it another way, Michael Schumacher may not be my mother, but my mother is definitely Michael Schumacher, and a little of Juan Fangio and partly Nelson Piquet.

156

The point is, she drives much too fast. This type is characterized by their underlying philosophy— we must reach yesterday.

They always assume they are running late, and are constantly in a state of mental panic. They tend to be abusive to those not in sync with their haste. These abuses range from 'you oaf' (used by my mother), to 'swinehund out of mine vey', which is prosaic German for 'swineherd out of my way'. The latter, of course, is used by the now retired Michael Schumacher and occasionally by both our mothers.

The second type is the 'slowly Gonzales' variety. This consists of a huge group of people such as the entire French nation, Christopher Columbus, my junior school principal, heads of state who apparently never have any agenda, and well, my father. This breed is the direct opposite to the first group. They are never in a hurry, always reach behind schedule, and can crawl right up the nose of the members from the first group with their long, arduous, and aimless meandering.

My father can take years to negotiate a turn, and it's not because of any lack of skill on his part. Columbus, on counsel, took years to get to his destination. And after all that, he got to the wrong place. This lack of drive ensures that these guys

157

are the catalyst for more altercations than both other groups put together.

The third group is known as the 'distracted Gonzales' variety. This group, which is most common in our modern times, does everything else while driving, but actually drive. They eat, answer phones, text messages, read emails, clean glasses or trade shares. Distracted by all these activities, they tend to go the wrong way up one-ways, jump signals, cut lines, and generally cause mayhem with alarming regularity. This group consists of all of the Japanese parts of South Korea, the entire world teenage population, and...err...how do I put this nicely...me. Both the other groups live in constant fear of this group. In fact, this is the most cannibalized group, as members of the group themselves are wary of other members. By the way, I'm writing this while driving, and truth be told, am making more headway with the writing, than with the driving.

To further elucidate my point, let's look at history. You may not know this but Hitler, while driving his Range Rover, was pushed off his lane and into a ditch by a distracted Gonzales ahead of him, who was trying to complete a puzzle while driving. The driver's name was Isaac Rubix. Hitler never recovered, and we all know how the world suffers till date because of all these Hitler impressionists with tumble German accents.

And the next time two countries go to war, remember it's your fault for driving too slowly.

159

Get one, get two free

Dear Mr Broacha,

My name is Jayant Patel. My uncle, Nalin Patel says he was in school with you, and apparently my maasi Jayshree Patel was one year senior to your sister, who by the way was in the same house as my cousin Deepali Patel, whose elder sister Ami Patel shares a birthday with your very own mother on November 25, though forty years apart.

Actually, I've been born and brought up in Canterbury, Kent in England. I've just moved back to Mumbai on a one-year transfer from my parent company. My mother is paranoid that I will catch a disease or two in this city. What diseases should I watch out for? (As a young boy I've already had malaria and mumps). My height is 177 cm and my weight is 73 kilos, and I'm a pure vegetarian, except on Sundays, when I eat onions due to the lack of any companion.

Yours kindly,

Jayant.

Dearest Jayant,

Of course I remember Nalin. He was the only boy in class who couldn't sit cross-legged on the floor. I wonder if they ever found a cure for that. Please convey my fond greetings to your uncle. And thank you for the family connection. Deepali was the first girl I ever asked for a dance and although she said no by stepping on my foot and shoving the back of my head into a hedge, I still think of her fondly.

Now, congratulations on landing an assignment in Mumbai, and I'm glad that both you and your mom are being overly cautious. As you are a vegetarian, we can straight away scratch out chicken pox, but I have made a list of available diseases with their suitable times:

a) measles is freely available first thing in the morning and more likely in the early part of the week

b) by mid-day, typhoid and paratyphoid are the most popular

c) late afternoon seems to be a favourite for both dengue and jaundice. Since dengue is not a resident and comes from abroad, jaundice should be a definite for you sooner or later

161

d) by evening you'd have consumed at least three meals, and the result will be amoebic dysentery, which will allow you to spend more quality time in the toilet. The amoeba apparently have a great affinity for non-resident Indians and once they get to you, they forge a relationship which lasts a lifetime—your lifetime that is

e) since you've already had malaria, you seem ripe for pneumonia in the late evening air

f) nightfall brings out the big boys such as gonorrhea and their fellow sexually transmitted cousins.

Then there is the whole gamut of unpronounceable diseases such as leptospirosis, Chikungunya, and St John's Wort. These are generally discouraged as they tend to trip on the Indian tongue. If you're looking at all this from a positive perspective, India, and Mumbai especially, has some disease or the other for everyone. All travellers to our country may freely avail themselves of these diseases. Jayant, if you stay true to form, you should land yourself three big ones in the course of your one year here.

And feel free to take one, anyone, perhaps your favourite one, back to England with you. Others have done the same and with spectacular results. I would like to add that Sir Robert Clive took syphilis back with him, Dalhousie took a whooping cough without the cold, and Stanley Cripps took the Pandey brothers, though one was lost at sea in a mysterious manner.

Paranoid travellers to India will tell you paranoid things such as avoid the food, water, and air. What they forget to tell you is if you avoid food, water, and air—you die. Wouldn't it be simpler to embrace a little cholera for a couple of months and continue to live, albeit a little suspiciously, for a few more months?

By the way, Jayant, my mother says Ami and her weren't more than forty years apart. In fact, her exact words were, 'What kind of mental disease is that whacko Jayant suffering from that he believes Ami and I were born forty years apart?' Jayant, I took the liberty of answering for you. I said, 'Jayant, hasn't got a mental disease yet, but he's applied for one.'

Anyhow, enjoy your stay in India. Remember to stay positive, and give my love to your extended family.

Warmly,

Cyrus.

P.S.: If it is at all possible, can you send me a picture of Nalin sitting cross-legged on the floor, if one is available that is, please?

Sister Act

Hello,

My name is Sam. Okay, you got me, my real name is Himanshu. But in New Jersey people tend to take hours over the name so I shortened it to 'Shu'. However, I soon got tired of the jokes and changed it to Sam. I've been living in the States for the past eleven years. Last month my cousin (Shyam Sundar aka Monty) got married in Goa at a plush five star hotel with its own beach. Here I was surrounded by some of my more backward cousins, and was witness to a most unpleasant sight.

A few of my female cousins, having never heard of the word swimsuit, let alone bikini, decided to go for a swim in the sea. This they did by remaining upright in chest-high water while still in their salwar kameezes (I must point out that I'm unfamiliar with the plural of salwar kameez). The end result was that when they emerged from the water, they created what experts today call, the parachute effect, that is the salwar kameezes were filled with air and water creating a balloon-like shape, which gives the wearer the appearance of a poorly made parachute as the top of their outfit. All my American friends who witnessed these elephantine apparitions come out of the water, doubled up with laughter with such force that they lost consciousness and had to be revived, with elaborate Ayurvedic procedures. I was so ashamed and dismayed at my cousins that I started talking with a Trinidadian accent, and to any foreigners who enquired where I was from I said, 'from the West Indies'.

My question to you is, how do I modernize these morons? Keep in mind that I can't keep up the Trinidad accent consistently especially when I speak in Punjabi. Like most Punjabis, my Punjabi too has a strong American accent.
Sam.

Dear Himanshu, a.k.a. Shu, a.k.a. Sam,

Accents are never easy, and one tends to get exposed sooner or later. So quite naturally, pretending you're not Indian, while clearly a sensible option, is not a long term solution. I think quite honestly you're barking up the wrong tree, scratching the other leg, wearing the wrong suit, or as the Trinidadians say, 'dropping the shrump off the Barbie'.

You see, Shu, sorry Sam...err...if I may, Sammy, we Indians are in a unique position. No other nationality can quite boast of our kind of disparity within just the one family, and here I'm talking not just financial, but social disparity. For example, you may have gone to a Swiss finishing school, but your cousin Piyush may think that Swiss is an 'omnipoetic' sound that one hears when a knife clashes with a fork on your plate.

In this particular example, I, too, have witnessed the parachute effect on a couple of occasions, and like the foreigners, I, too, had trouble controlling my convulsions and bodily fluids. Few sights in nature could be rated as funny as women in inflated salwar kameez or kameezes, emerging from the sea. Although the penguins' mating ritual would come quite close. Coming back to my first point, Sam, I think you need to change your perspective. Instead of educating and modernizing your 'moronic', as you yourself put it, relatives, I think you need to celebrate their backwardness. Imagine if you had advertised to all your foreign friends about the sight that they would see in India. No one would have believed you. Yet on seeing the

167

real thing, your hype would have been more than justified, and you'd have been treated as a god by your foreign peers. The guys would have put you on a pedestal because you were the guy with quirky relatives.

So, Shu…err…Sam, simply turn this whole issue to your advantage. Play the role of ring master or impresario, and if you can't spell impresario stick to ring master. It's just a question of being mastered by your relatives or being a master to them.

By the way, you said the hotel had its own enclosed beach. Can you tell me which hotel it was, as I have a few relatives of my own…ones which, quite frankly, I can't really be seen with in public.

Yours sincerely,

Cyrus.

168

Dr Bhajeewala (PhD)

Hi Cyrus,

This is Vijay Singh Badal (V.S.B.) this side. I hope it is Cyrus that side. Recently, I attended a workshop in Boston. As you know, Boston is a very famous city that side. In the workshop as I was representing India, I was asked 'Who is the most intellectual male in India?' Or to make it easier for you, 'Who is the smartest man, this side?'

I have narrowed down the list to our spiritual bodies, politicians, nuclear scientists, and of course writers, yourself included.

Please give me your expert opinion.

From my side,

Vijay Singh Badal.

Dear V.S.B.

No, Vijay Singh Badal, no. Your list from your side is most erroneous. None of those worthies that you have mentioned compare to the actual intellectual giant of Asia. I'm sure by now you've realized the error of your ways and guessed the answer for yourself. India's greatest intellectual is, and always will be, the vegetable vendor. Or to give him his full name, the Bhajeewala (Bhajeewala loosely translates from the original Latin of Bhaja 'vege' and 'wala' which means man. Very few people are aware of this).

The Bhajeewala's intelligence is exactly like the Rottweiler's ferocity. Four instant truths spring to mind when we examine the everyday, common garden variety of Bhajeewalas:

a) all Bhajeewalas look exactly the same

b) all Bhajeewalas have an assistant Bhajeewala who will in turn become the main Bhajeewala once the senior Bhajeewala feels he's sold his last Bhajee

c) as a follow up to Truth (a)—all assistant Bhajeewalas look exactly like the senior Bhajeewalas

d) all Bhajeewalas suffer from both hernia and rheumatoid arthritis, due to the nature of their work, that is, lifting very heavy objects such as cucumbers, spinach, and French bean without wearing any undergarment at the time.

Now let's examine an actual display of intelligence at work.

Mrs Mathur, who herself looks like a ladyfinger breeding experiment gone awry from the neck down, approaches a Bhajeewala on the street.

The lady in question will now be starting a long selection process to find the right cucumber. In this, she will elicit help from the only man who knows more about the cucumber than the cucumber itself.

She will first start with less important questions. I have tried to translate this conversation from the original Hindi, and it may most definitely lose something in the translation.

Mrs Mathur: Good man, how much for some fresh cucumber?

Good man: Rs 75 a kilo.

Mrs Mathur: Do you share the cerebral matter of a primate such as a mandrill or a baboon?

Good man: No.

Mrs Mathur: Then if your brain has finally cleared up, tell me the real price?

Good man: Rs 22 a kilo, but for this you must also stop calling me a baboon repeatedly in public.

Mrs Mathur: Done. Now, my good man, can you, using your special native gifts, feel and tell me which is your most succulent cucumber?

171

And this is where the actual intelligence, the mind-boggling ability takes over.

The Bhajeewala proceeds to pick up a variety of cucumbers. Some he discards like a hot rash. Some he caresses while some he holds. Some he puts to his ear. But the one he finally selects is put through a wholly different process. He holds up the cucumber in one hand so it catches the sunlight, then with his free hand he proceeds to knock on it. Just like one would knock on a door. He does it so convincingly that you'd expect the cucumber to open at any moment.

After this is done, he proceeds to attempt to shove the large cucumber up his right nostril. After three futile attempts, he presents the cucumber to Mrs Mathur. She in turn astutely realizes there isn't enough space in her nostril for both a nose ring and a cucumber. The Bhajeewala's expertise has however worked its charm on Mrs Mathur, and she wants to adopt both the cucumber and the Bhajeewala. But then she realizes that Mr Mathur may be threatened by the arrival of a second cucumber and abandons the plan.

Vijay Singh Badal, you and I have learnt a very important lesson here today. First, you really can't put a cucumber in your nose, and secondly that no one can understand a vegetable, the way it is,

172

the way it breathes, the way it eats, its height, weight, colour, its mood swings, wants, ambitions, aspirations, its feelings, and insecurities like the Bhajeewala.

A research lab spends millions of dollars, hires super educated scientists, fits them with the latest in equipment technology and occasionally running shorts, yet this multi-million dollar franchise can't tell you for sure which cucumber is the most succulent, even if you gave them six months to do so. The Bhajeewala can answer this question in thirty-six seconds.

Aryabhatta gave us the zero, but could he give a succulent cucumber? Einstein handed over relativity to us, but did he even once mention the cucumber? Ramanujan could put any numbers together, but could he put together a cucumber?

I don't think so.

So there you have it, the answer to your question. In the words of India's greatest poet Faiz A. Faiz, 'cucumber da jawab nahi!'

Love,

Cyrus.

173

Book Two

The Incoherent Thoughts of an Average Indian Male

It's time to move on to Book Two. Why Book Two, you ask preciously. Let me answer your query on two accounts:

a) I know the answer

b) there actually is no one else here.

All great books come in two parts. And I'm sure you will agree with me when I tell you that up to page 7, clearly this had the makings of a great book. Anyhow as I said, all great books come in two parts. The French call these Part I and Part II. But who really cares about the French? The books are more likely divided by the names 'prequel', then 'sequel' and finally the...err... 'threequel'. In this particular book, the prequel has dealt with letters and professional thoughts, and now we have the sequel which tackles things on a holistic level. What does one know about the term holistic except that you do not spell it with a 'w'?

Now that we have set up the perimeters, it's time to put the ball in play. This book started out as a guide to the Indian male, but by page 17.5 it lost interest and veered towards author's facets of Indianness, and now it's moving into a travelogue area. In short, Book Two can easily be mistaken for a *National Geographic* magazine, except, of course, for one simple fact: our book has much better pictures.

176

So what makes a male in Kozhikode tick? How is he different from a male in Ghaziabad? And how do you spell Kozhikode in the first place? Are the mating habits of Sector 17 in Chandigarh similar to the habits in Pakmodia Street in Mumbai? Who can tie their shoelaces faster, the people in the east or those in the north? Has a male rickshawalla in Bengaluru historically ever actually adhered to a red light and stopped his vehicle? Are there really Punjabis in space? Lastly, who has the worst exercise routine, the Bengali or the Gujarati? And the most important ecological question of our time, who leaves the maximum amount of footwear in our holy Ganges?

All these questions may or may not be answered (this depends largely on the author's mood) but there we are, dear reader. Book Two tries to do a Tiger Woods. That is, to plug…err…all the holes.

Whoever you are, male or female, adult or child, tall or short, at the end of this book if you've paid attention or dozed off no more than three times while turning these pages, you will have the most comprehensive understanding of the Indian male and the Indian subcontinent as well.

The Indian male after all, is only a speck on this great Indian landscape. Although don't tell him that, because, off the record, he has a huge complex about the issue of size. Be that as it may, now that we've set the bar higher, let's plunge into Book Two with a voracious thirst for knowledge. A thirst which only the second part of a great book can provide. I'd like to close with an old advertising maxim, not because of any particular relevance here, but purely because I just remembered it. Anything is possible with Nikki-Tasha Kitchenette.

Memories
(not from the musical *Cats*)

One of my most vivid memories from childhood is my father's one–to–one (man to another man) talks. Plenty of sons in many parts of the world probably share this same ritual with their fathers of course.

Our talks normally centered around something epic, something monumental, something gargantuan in nature, like for instance when he forgot his wife's anniversary, and called me in for a talk session as he desperately needed a favour. I for my part refused to hide him, as a matter of principle. Keep in mind, an 11-year-old generally fears repercussions from an already furious mom far more than weak threats from a convulsing, writhing, shivering pater.

Then, there was always the talk to do with a tragedy. Tragic news is normally conveyed by the father to son, like the time he took me aside to tell me some particularly grave news. I still remember as the words, 'David Gower has been dropped from the 1993 England tour to India', hit me. I felt weak in the knees, and had to be helped to my seat by an already crestfallen dad.

Then, obviously, there's also the visionary news, the statement of intent. Of all the father-son talks, these are the ones that absolutely left that indelible mark for posterity. For instance, one day, my father gestured to me 'the gesture'. The gesture was the hidden code, known to everyone in the house and the immediate neighbourhood, that meant he and I should retire to another room for our father and son chat with immediate effect. The gesture itself was very subtle and had been a few generations in the making. This gesture comprised of my father raising four fingers over each ear, while simultaneously rolling his eyes round and round till they looked like giant saucers and coughing violently at the same tune. Actually the coughing wasn't part of the gesture, but just a residual effect of sixty-four cigarettes a day, which ensured a coughing fit roughly over every twenty-two seconds whilst awake and every forty-six seconds whilst asleep.

Once we both had made it to the communications headquarters, also known as the closest available room, my dad began, 'Son it's time to make a life altering decision. One that once made cannot be reversed. One that has the power to alter one's destiny, one's future, and one's very life itself. It's the same decision Julius Caesar had to make on whether to cross the Rubicon river. The same sort of decision Luciano Pavarotti had to make when he had to decide whether to skip dessert in order to lose the 16 pounds or so required to get into his Paglinchi (like in the opens) down costume for the grand reopening of La Scala Milan.'

At this point in the father and son talk, my father had metamorphosed into a general addressing his troops before battle. His hand gestures were faster than a Bengaluru traffic cop and his decibel level meant that by now everybody in the surrounding five buildings were privy to the chat.

'Son, what is that you see on the chair?' So saying my father pointed to a collection of his old underwear collected on a chair.

'Medieval underwear,' I replied, aiming to be more factual than flippant.

My father picked up one from the pile—a hideous purple with a disfigured band—and

181

hanging elastic threads. The years of disuse gave it a more cardboard than cotton look.

'The time has come to give up underwear.' He proclaimed.

I was shocked, this announcement was going the David Gower way. I mean, I was no great fan of underwear. But to give it up completely...let's face it, *Free Willy* works for two hours, no more.

No underwear! That would be a monumental change, a cultural shift, far too drastic. It could shake the very foundation of our society, bring down the bedrock that is our civilization. No underwear, indeed!

'Change is inevitable,' continued my father.

I immediately fainted. For standing in front of me, was my father in boxer shorts and nothing else. His thin, lily white legs, which had never seen the sun, were dwarfed by an oversized pair of boxers that worked quite clearly like a plastic bag hanging around the privates. A plastic bag with very nice embroidery. A constellation of stars chasing the seven dwarfs with Snow White smiling in the background. As I stood there amazed and aghast, in that order, the man in the plastic bag with Dopey in front and centre continued. 'The whole world is moving away from traditional underwear to free flowing boxers, I suggest we do the same...'

Let's leave my father there, ranting about the glory that is boxer shorts, and how both Caesar and Pavarotti were the first to experiment with them. Oh, by the way, if you are one of the few people who've seen us in our birthday suits, you know why we male Broachas are today part plastic bag.

What followed, of course, was a world movement, which divided men on three sides. Those who wore the traditional underwear, those who wore boxers, and those who just didn't wear any form of underwear. The three groups can't co-exist, they are bound to clash, and while no one can tell the future, it seems abundantly clear that the next Great World War will not be fought over trivial things such as religion, land, or ethnicity, but indeed over the issues of type of underwear.

183

Status (not the Udipi restaurant)

In the entire history of the world, which begins with Hammurabi and ends with the formation of Bangladesh (Hammurabi Public Relations people would like to add that he has nothing to do with nor does he approve of a separate state for Bangladesh), has there ever been a country as superstitious as our own.

If you observe the average Indian male, you'll see him showing obeisance when he passes any house of worship. Then there is that strange act of touching a cow and then touching one's head as a mark of respect. This could mean one of two things—you want to show genuine respect and reverence to the cow or you want the cow to replace your own head.

Bovine experts say that the cow does not particularly enjoy this act. Cows don't particularly enjoy being touched by members of other species too, especially when they are ovulating. I mean, let's face it, other species have much more sense. When was the last time you saw a gorilla touch a cow for that matter? And, if by chance a tiger touches a cow, the cow is generally never heard of again. It's just us, with our strange habits, that perform rituals that make sense to us and us alone.

Then there's that other act of touching the feet of elders. Americans don't do this. For the Canadians, it's a strict no-no. And for Germans, it's generally considered an act of war. No elderly European wants to be reminded of his age, especially by some young buck faking immense concern. In the animal kingdom, it's well nigh impossible for a young polar bear to touch a senior polar bear's foot. And if he does so by mistake, he better run for his life with immediate effect.

Yet for us Indians, the scene is played out again and again. Young man goes to meet elderly relatives. He rings the doorbell and senior relative greet him at the door. Now young man makes as if he's diving towards his elder's feet, but in actuality he just does a six-inch bend, whereupon senior relative grabs his shoulders and pulls him back up, while simultaneously checking the youngster's scalp for the inevitable bald spot so that he can laugh about this privately later. But the question here is, why do we have these superstitions and why keep these customs for over forty-thousand years?

The answer is complex. Not complexed, just complex. That is, superiority complex. Our civilization was built not on the tenets of egalitarianism and equality, but on a simple principle called 'know your place'.

'Know your place' is like a game—when an Indian meets a fellow Indian, we immediately decide to adopt an inferior or superior stance. A fellow Indian is either below you or above you in the social scale, never equal. Let's look at this chart. Father/mother, above you. Children, below you. Mr Sharma, your neighbour, who is older, above you. Mrs Sharma who is younger, below you.

A pigeon, below you. A cow, above you. A God you've heard of, definitely above you. A God you haven't heard of, still above you. A normal building, below you. A religious structure, above you. The sun, moon, and stars, above you. People in a village in the Sunderbans, below you. A minister of the government, in public above you, in private, way below you. Your driver, below you. A famous driver like Lewis Hamilton, above you. A bowl of food, above you. A bowl of food, without any food, below you.

This list is very long and only Indians are privy to the entire list. Yet the explanation is sound. Due to the 'know your place' theory, we form relationships on the basis of extra respect or no respect.

For example, my publisher is above me, however sadly, you dear reader…well, why go on about it, I think we are both fairly clear about the status.

Tony
(not mother of Banta)

Years ago, and I mean at least twenty-five or more years ago, Aryabhatta invented the zero. Let's put this in perspective. Aryabhatta, or Tony as he was known to guys on his street, was an avid scientist. He didn't just invent the zero. He also invented many other numbers such as seven, twenty-two, and possibly even the number three. His inventions, of course, didn't stop there. He is said to have invented, among other things, collared shirts, polka dots, the Raspberry Ripple, and the opening chords of 'Sultans of Swing'. None of these made much of an impact. But his zero, on the other hand, changed India forever.

Few may know this, but before the advent of the zero, Indian society was extremely efficient and disciplined as both the sun dial and the sand clock were very popular. Back then, Indians were often mistaken for Germans because they were extremely punctual and fastidious when it came to executing things. Then came Aryabhatta's zero. It came, it saw, and it conquered. As the zero got sucked into the system it started corrupting it, much like a virus. The zero is based on the concept of nothingness, and in the world of nothingness, there is, of course, no time. This nothingness philosophy flew thick and fast, and the mighty Indians started slowing down. A road from ancient Pataliputra to modern day Mussoorie, which should have been completed in seven months, is yet to be completed. Suddenly, Indian efficiency was affected forever. Such was the power of Aryabhatta's zero. How one wishes we had taken to his collared shirts or polka dots in the same way instead.

Years later, if there is one criticism you can nail against us Indians, it is poor time management. We just can't do anything on time. And I experienced this as a young boy when I came into contact with my friend and neighbour Ayaan.

It was widely known as The Mystery of Ayaan. After waking up, there was no record of what Ayaan did. All we knew is that whatever he did, he would never be ready on time. Every single day Ayaan would miss the school bus. This by itself was not without parallels. But what happened next still boggles the

189

mind. Every afternoon he would miss the bus back home as well. What exactly did Ayaan do? Why was he always late? Why couldn't he change? These questions soon replaced the regular ones in our text books such as, 'What's the capital of Nigeria?', 'Who built the Gol Gumbaz and when?', and 'What came first, sine, cos, or theta?' By the way, don't confuse cos, sine, beta, with coze, fan, tutti, the latter is a Mozart opera, and far more difficult to understand.

Finally, it was proved that Ayaan spent more time in trying to get to school and trying to get home from school, than actual time spent in school. And what did Ayaan do that caused all those delays? The answer lies in Aryabhatta's genius—he did nothing. Zilch, nada, or as we put it today, zero. Ayaan, even at that young age, was wise beyond his age and had embraced the concept of nothingness. The soul of Aryabhatta glowed brightly, albeit in a delayed fashion, in Ayaan.

We all have Ayaans in our life. They are never ready when you pick them up. They never reach the appointed restaurant on time. They can single-handedly destroy group dynamics. This they do by changing the moods of the different members of the group, until they are at each other's throats.

Coming back to the source of all the Ayaans of our world, is the irresponsible Tony (Aryabhatta). I, for one, am immediately stripping Aryabhatta of

190

his Dronacharya award. (Keep in mind that this was the only time that the Dronacharya award was presented by Dronacharya himself).

Where is the grass? (not the kind on a lawn)

People often stop me on the road. Most of them do that just so that they can pass by in peace. Some though, ask me this fabulous question (and mind you, it is always the same question)—'where can I score some?'

I can't quite say why they do this, because I'm not your typical drug pusher. I crop my hair short, I don't sport a beard and occasionally shower, and I rarely dress in more than four colours. Really, I have no idea why they do this. It could be that I have an approachable face or that I look like one of the world's most famous drug pushers from Columbia (yes, I do get asked in Spanish sometimes), and a few people think it's because I wear a shirt which says 'I grow marijuana', followed by an arrow sign pointing nether region ways.

I don't grow marijuana and certainly not where the arrow points. Also I'd like to point out that most Indians can't pronounce marijuana, forget trying to spell it, and those on marijuana most definitely cannot spell it, as various test studies have shown. Yet my altruistic nature, my 'how can I please you' personality (a personality that I share with Oskar Schindler, Florence Nightingale, and Mother Teresa) makes it very difficult for me to turn anyone away. So, when I'm asked, I genuinely try to help.

You have to understand, however, that I'm not for a minute condoning the flippant use of narcotics or rather, substance abuse. I'm merely answering questions, much as one would answer a terrorist who is asking for the address of the nearest train station. After all, by doing so, I am merely telling the truth. And at the primary school level, in all cultures and all lands, aren't we all told again and again that we must tell the truth, the whole truth, and nothing but the truth? Similarly, when one is asked a question, one must answer truthfully. So you ask me about drugs, I'll tell you about drugs. You ask me about train stations, again I'll tell you about train stations. And if you ask me my pan card number, I'll tell you about train stations again.

Now when it comes to drugs, it's generally, first, a geographical question. Where? I immediately, to the best of my knowledge, guide the prospective customer. This I do by drawing a map explaining how to get to the…err…the drug store. I then list seven or eight phone numbers, emails, and details of the closest male relative of the area's finest and most respected narcotics suppliers.

If this is still not satisfactory I provide them with information which is more detailed—photographs of the pushers in various states of undress, photographs of the pushers with various religious figures, copies of their birth certificates, blood group, and urine and stool samples. Mind you, I have to stress again that I don't use, sell, or consume drugs in any form. I just answer their questions because of years of classical conditioning that forbids me to tell an untruth.

The link now is exceedingly clear. Drugs are bad, a bane on society, a catalyst for all kinds of evil. We have to rid our society of drugs. And there is only one way to do it. We have to destroy the root cause—schools. If we tear down our schools, no one will teach us this messy business of telling the truth, and no one will guide prospective clients to these dens of drugs that derange and destroy people. Schools have to become extinct, and the truth must be reversed. There is no other way. I know you may not like what you're reading, but forgive me, I'm just another hopeless victim of education.

The clap (not the kind that is sexually transmitted)

Intrepid traveller Fa-Hein (who also went by the English name Mickey whenever in Europe), spent a great deal of time in India, in between jobs. He made his own general observations about the people he met. And although he fathered four children with three different Indian women, he always felt a great disconnect with this ancient civilization. His biggest grouse was that people didn't like to look him in the eye (although to be absolutely frank, if he was to lay the cards on the table, this may have something to do with the fact that Fa-Hein was perfectly hideous to look at), and that in spite of the fact that most of the communication was done using hands, Indians rarely like to applaud. Fa-Hein wrote three books, *Murder in the Cathedral*,

King Solomon's Mines, and *Before the Fat Lady Sings*, all about his travels through India. In all three, he talks of how he felt when Indians around him refused to clap. In Chapter 4, page 7 of *Murder in the Cathedral*, Fa-Hein tells a sad tale.

'At my very first discourse held at the village fair four kilometres outside Bhubaneshwar, I pulled in a crowd of 470 people. I remember thinking to myself that would be 469 more than I would ever pull in China, and after my mother's death that number would go back to minus 470. Happy with the turnout, inspite of the fact that none in the audience were wearing trousers, I began my speech with great gusto. I always start the same way. That day was no different. My opening is always the crack about the Chinese guy, the Mesopotamian guy, and the Indian guy at the bar...I declared a smashing rendition of the joke, but when I got to the final line, I got the same response I always get in India—no applause, just unblinking stares. To be honest, I get a better response at funerals. I was so taken aback, I started spitting at the crowd. But instead of attacking me, their response was just the same—stares, cold, unblinking, meaningless stares. No applause, no participation, yet oddly no one left the gathering. It was like performing for the damned or worse, the dead.

197

I immediately made a mental note to make changes in the second half of my act, which by the way, includes some of the juiciest items such as my Cantonese stand-up act; my one-legged lambada, and my one-voice, fourteen harmonies repertoire that never fails to elicit a riotous response. I couldn't help wondering what (Chinese expletive) is wrong with these (Chinese double expletive) people?'

So what is wrong with us? Why don't we respond by clapping? Why aren't we more participative or appreciative? If you look around and observe the average Indian, say that guy over there...yes, him, you will notice how his hands play a very important role in his life. If he tries to greet you, he'll use both his hands. Farewell is similar, so much so that foreigners don't leave as they are unable to distinguish between the two gestures.

When an Indian wants to say thanks, he raises his hands (palms upward) above his head. Keep in mind, Indians compulsorily include God in their thank you. Similarly, hands convey the order 'come', 'go', 'you come', 'I'll go', 'up', 'down', 'you have something in your hair' and much more. An Indian without his hands is akin to a Frenchman without his French. So why don't we use the obviously much-used hands to clap?

198

The answer, I'm afraid, is in the last sentence. Okay not the last sentence from this sentence but the last sentence from two sentences before. If you, of course, count this sentence. We don't show appreciation by clapping simply because we've over-used the hands from the time we Indians wake up and wash our behinds till the time we sleep at night after our 194th interaction with God. All this hand talk means something's got to give. Somewhere down the line, we have to put our hands up and say, 'No more hands'. This normally manifests itself at a public performance, a speech, a recital, or even somebody else's grand gesture. At all these moments when we should show appreciation with our hands, we, instead, take a break from the hand stuff and substitute it with the blank Indian unblinking stare. Today, that stare is the accepted measure for appreciation used by our people. So if you are a performer or just an average do-gooder, don't, I repeat, don't wait for the claps.

Now, between you and me, Fa-Hein's case was a little different. The people didn't respond to him, didn't clap for him for one reason, and one reason alone—he spoke in Chinese.

Author's note: Actually there is no such thing as he spoke in Chinese, just as there is no such thing as he spoke in Indian. At that time the poorer sections of Chinese society spoke Cantonese. Fa-Hein came from the richer sections, and spoke, as all rich Chinese then did, French.

Pedestrian (not to be confused with my writing style)

As a social commentator, one of my many jobs is to observe the traits of us Indians. Unique, distinct traits such as nodding our heads continuously, consistent unhygenic behaviour in public toilets, and checking the cricket score. Over a large period of time (okay, okay, since 6:30 this evening), I've observed a strange aversion among our city folk. We are all afraid of pavements.

According to scientists, Singh and Swaminathan (who chronically tragically lost their lives when a garbage disposal truck ran over them twice as they crossed the road), this fear of pavements is known as pavement phobia, and is limited to the people of this subcontinent. Next time you're crossing a road, look around you. First you will see a road teeming with cars, then in the middle of this stream of cars you'll see people, Indian people, walking about exactly as if they were in their living rooms. Some stop cars with their hands while they cross, some just ignore the cars as if they weren't even there in the first place. Some actually think they are the cars, and are absolutely convinced, without a shadow of doubt, that the cars are the pedestrians. Not a single human being is to be found on the smooth surfaced, abundant pavement that lies on either side of the road, and if at all one is found, it would turn out to be a visiting German or Japanese diplomat.

The crossing laid out at the junction of various roads across India holds a unique record. They have never been used by a human being. Stray dogs, occasionally yes, pigeons once or twice maybe, flies on public holidays definitely, but never ever by human beings. Pavements and crossings are found all across India, but like Michael Jackson's women, they have never been touched. The question you must ask here is why? Why have Michael Jackson's women never been touched? Also why don't we use the damn public pavements and crossings?

Singh and Swaminathan, God rest their souls, have an insight to this phenomenon. It's to do, again, with our genes. We Indians have a short cut gene.

This is a gene which forces us to always choose an easier and quicker option to obstacles in our path. Let's play back a situation. Check this out.

The other day you're walking in the park, minding your own business, when a large elephant walks into your path. Do you:

a) go back the way you came?
b) charge at the elephant?
c) quickly show the elephant a picture of Lady Gaga on your mobile phone which causes the elephant to go into ovulation. Which is a particularly strange phenomenon as the elephant is male.
d) wet your pants?

The correct answer, if you're being true to yourself and if you're an Indian passport holder, is you'd obviously bend over backwards, clasp your ankles with your hands, thus convincing the elephant that you're, in fact, a toadstool. Then when the elephant's not looking, you'd cross to the other end of the park, where the exit is and waddle your way back home before the wife finds you in a compromising position with an elephant. This you will a 100 percent do because of your short cut gene—a consequence of your Indianness. The result would have been different if you were a Westerner. An American would have tried to chat up the elephant, while a European would have taken one step further and mounted her. This would have led to a terrible situation as we all know that an Indian elephant's standards are very high.

But is there any solution in sight? Again, let us turn to Singh and Swaminathan, who immediately would in turn, turn away. So let me instead take up the cudgels on their behalf (God rest their souls), and once again wear my social commentator's hat, along with a blue pin-stripe suit and a fetching red tie. The answer is, yet again, in the short cut theory.

There is no point trying to convince pedestrians to use long winding pavements and crossings, but there is a lot of sense in asking cars to move out of the roads and get onto the pavements. Once on the comfort of a pavement, a car will never have to use a horn again, as it will never ever again encounter a pedestrian. Cars will get smoother, non-obstacled courses to drive on, and pedestrians can claim their birthright to road after road in peace. See, with just a tweak here and there we can all live together...in peace. You may think that I'm short changing you with this answer. But if you want a more complex, longwinded, thorough one, just wait till I get my green card.

Phamily phrend (English translation of phamily phrend)

As a young boy, like was the case in most families in India, one had to get used to three sets of acquaintances. The first set was your own friends, the second your relatives who, no matter how much you tried, could not be returned, and the third was the family friends. The third case is almost uniquely Indian, and it consists of friends acquired by your own family, namely your mother and father, hundreds of years ago. These family friends are then thrust upon you, and you have to remain absolute friends with them for life, as a result of an absurd social contract engineered by your parents, which was done behind your back and without consulting you, on the flimsiest of grounds that you weren't born at the time.

Under no conditions could you miss a family friend's dinner. No excuse would be allowed for trying to bunk a family friends' gathering. Pregnancy and career be damned. If a family friend's evening had been announced, you better be there come hell or highwater.

The trouble was that the 'family friends' were not always on one's wavelength. Take the Kapoors for example. They consisted of five people— Colonel Mohinder Kapoor, who preferred to be called Monty; Heena Kapoor, who only spoke about Monty, her husband; Nandita Kapoor, who thought for some reason that the three pig-tail format was back in fashion; Tarun Kapoor, who was raised on a strict diet of only jalebis, and which explained why at just age 11 he was four kilos heavier than his own father. The fifth member was, of course, Monty Kapoor's moustache, roughly the size and shape of a boomerang which sprang across his face from ear to ear. The amount of time Monty spent grooming it and talking about it, made it abundantly clear that this was his favourite child.

As family friends go; these were the ones I wanted to avoid the most. They topped my list of 'people you don't want to ever have contact with', and keep in mind that I was only 8 at

206

the time and had not evolved into the super prejudiced bigoted savage that I'm now proud to call myself.

First and foremost, Heena Kapoor could only discuss her husband. She seemed to be just another extension of him, another moustache if you will. And she had this terrible habit of consistently patting my hair down while simultaneously bobbing her chin to her chest. She just wouldn't let up, and this unnecessary form of contact would go on for hours. She also had this disagreeable 'n' sound that she'd produce while grinding her teeth. This would emanate after every sentence spoken by her husband that worked like a reinforcing effect. For example, Col. Kapoor would say, 'In the 1971 war, I found myself alone against nine Pakistani soldiers. Nine Pakistani soldiers.'

Even as he finished the sentence Heena would emit the 'n' sound while grinding her teeth, bobbing her chin, and patting my hair down.

Nandita was at the age where she spoke to no one and always carried a book with her. Only instead of age appropriate books such as the Nancy Drew series, she'd be reading *Paradise Lost* or *The Divine Comedy*. And her books always had titles with rather large lettering, so as to enable you to spot the title from at least forty yards away.

Tarun, who frighteningly looked exactly like a cricket sight screen, was actually the friendliest. The problem was, because of his shapelessness, you couldn't be seen with him, as his presence always triggered off sneers, and in some cases rhythmic laughter followed by difficulties in breathing.

That brings us to the Colonel, my father's own college friend. My father once told me how he wasn't really a colonel, although he had spent six months in the Merchant Navy. In spite of the Colonel basing his very existence on a lie, my father was very fond of him. Although he made sure he never referred to him as Colonel.

So at the family friends' dinner, Monty would talk about a war he never participated in and the length of his moustache, while his wife would make encouraging, if primitive, sounds behind him. The daughter would pretend to be reading a book, or at least make sure her entire face was covered by a book nobody could completely get through without the use of a heavy dose of illegal narcotics. The son would tuck into all the available food, and single-handedly dispose of all things sweet. My own parents would humour the Colonel and pretend to believe his tall tales while quietly collecting the empty bowls from his son. As for me and my sister, we were occupied by the only thing which could be called fascinating at the family friends' evening—we'd sit and stare at Monty's moustache in the hope that it would fall off and sort of metaphorically expose the whole family.

Sadly though, years later I found out that Monty's moustache outlived Monty. By a month!

Four-legged friend (not the same as a friend on crutches)

Mahatma Gandhi once said (and I paraphrase because he never said it to me), a society is judged by the way they treat their animals. Well, the relationship can do with some improving as we have killed most of ours. After the last count, we had four tigers, seven lions, two flamingoes, and a black bear suffering from scabies left. That's it.

Oh yes, we do have two species still doing all right—dogs and cows.

Dogs first. Dogs, for those of you who don't know, also go by the Greek term 'canine' or the Latin 'four-legged friend'. They are faithful and loyal companions who love to be the centre of all attention by indulging in their favourite sport, which is licking one's own genitalia. For this ability and this ability alone, Indians, especially Indian men, actually look up to dogs.

Dogs are also one of the few species who proudly carry their country's name in their own title such as the British Bull dogs or the Rhodesian Ridgeback or the German Shepherd or the Irish Wolfhounds. Of course, this works both ways, as in the case of the Afghan Hound, which is seeing dwindling popularity on account of her country's poor human rights record.

The relationship between dogs and Indians is a little frail and ambiguous. Indian literature and pop culture is filled with negative representation of canine phrases such as 'die like a dog' or 'you damn dog', or 'you are exactly equal to a dog', which are overused. This is in sharp contrast with our old scriptures, which provided more positive 'dog' references. For example, turn to page 32 of the Kama Sutra, and check out 'doggy style'. Nothing uncomplimentary there... For the Indian populace, their relationship with dogs follow four golden rules:

a) all dogs should be spoken to in English
b) all dogs should be called either Tommy, Raju, or Moti
c) dogs should power many outside their caste, under any circumstance

211

d) you can love your own dog, yet hate everybody else's, and still be called a dog lover.

Cows, of course, got the plum pose. If dogs form parts of the cabinet, then the cow is your prime minister. A cow, first and foremost, is holy. Which again means three things:

a) she can live anywhere
b) she doesn't have to wear clothes
c) she doesn't have to pay taxes.

Also if you're in a hurry and can't reach a mandir on time, all you need to do is touch Her Holiness, who acts as a walking holy place, albeit an extremely slow moving one. If a cow is in the middle of the road, you may not move her. You simply have to wait till she decides to move out of your way, a process which normally takes three to eight months.

The cow may not be used for food, physical relations, show jumping, cross country races, and furniture. In short, cows have it made. Dogs have to struggle, and for the rest of the animal kingdom it's all downhill and one-way traffic. Of the species with sizeable populations left, each has one strong and credible complaint. Crows and monkeys feel they are treated harshly at picnics. Pigeons want to have a more equal share in air conditioners.

212

Horses want a day off. Spiders want to come out of the closets. And bats would love a say in day light saving time.

Will any animal survive extinction in the next few years? Unfortunately, the correct answer to this may be in the last words of Maharana Pratap's best friend and four-legged companion Chetak, who ended his life with this immortal phrase, 'Neigh'.

Girls bar bar

My wife is planning my son's birthday party. And in keeping with our holy tradition and long practiced culture, her husband is the last to know.

My son Mikhaail is a lovely boy (on occasion) who wears his pants on his chest and has now started to wear sweaters even in 40° temperature. A feat performed successfully only by sheep and the latter-day Rishi Kapoor.

And although I'm the last to know, I've been rested assured (I know it is grammatically incorrect) that the bill would be arriving bang on time.

The birthday party is to be held nine days before the actual birthday. There are two reasons for this: (a) because my son wants to (b) because it allows him to celebrate his birthday twice.

The other request my son apparently put down to his mother scared the pants off me. His exact words were 'no girls'. For a father of a young son, these words can cut you to the bone. It is exactly the feeling George Michael got when he was released from jail early, against his best wishes.

With a few hours to go before the actual party, which is to be a football party, I put my son on my lap and tried to reason with him. But have you sometimes got that feeling that your 7-year-old is actually an 11-year-old? Well, sitting on my lap was one of those times, so we changed positions, sat on separate chairs, and I started the interrogation.

Cyrus: So, son, why?

Mikhaail: Why what?

Cyrus: Not why what, just why?

Mikhaail: Just why what?

Cyrus: No. Not just why what.

Realizing this was going nowhere, I decided to change tactics and become more confrontational.

Cyrus: Mikhaail, d'you like girls?

Mikhaail: Dad, d'you like girls?

Cyrus: I asked you first, but if you must know, I LOVE girls.

Mikhaail: Good. Good. When I grow up and get girls, I'll turn them over to you.

(I made a mental note of reminding him about his statement later in life).

Cyrus: But why don't you like girls?

Mikhaail: Many reasons. They smell. They have long hair. They gossip all the time, and they are stronger than me.

Cyrus: These are good reasons.

Mikhaail: Besides, in my class they all have the same name.

Cyrus: Which name?

Mikhaail: Anya.

Okay, I said to myself, these were good enough reasons. I then told my son the problem. The truth as I saw it. How when we age, we start wanting girls at our parties. First we just want a few of them. Then we feel at least half the party should be girls, and by the time you're 14, you're wishing the whole party was made up of girls only. Forget party! You hope the cake is a girl. The candles are girls, the decorations are girls, and the games girls. I tried to make him see the light. As one ages, inviting girls to birthdays becomes more and more difficult. The reasons for which are:

a) your mother will object
b) your wife will object
c) the girls themselves will object.

So one birthday without girls is one birthday wasted. One easy, girl-filled birthday that you can never claim back in later life. However, my son was adamant; my better sense, as usual, didn't prevail. My wife, of course, pushed the 'no girl' agenda. As my son secretly put it, 'She's a girl. If she approves a no-girl zone, then she obviously knows how dangerous girls can be.' Again a good reason. I could see his point.

But years later, when the boy is a man and he has to get up every day and pretend to work, when he's actually spending every waking moment checking out, thinking about, and talking to girls, he'll remember his father's words of wisdom and think he should have invited the GIRLS!

Olfactory disasters (don't necessarily happen in all factories)

Of all God's inventions, there's one that baffles me. Yet it has a wide reach, affecting all of us. Body odour, according to a letter published by the W.H.O., is a much faster growing menace than terrorism and affects more people than even acne does in today's global age.

Let me explain a few facts about body odour. Body odour is, contrary to what people think, a living thing. It is clearly male; no female could smell this bad. Body odour cannot be created or destroyed, but can be passed on from one person or thing to another (keep in mind that occasionally a person and a thing can be one and the same, as is the case with my own uncle Bestem). Body odour and sweating are not one and the same. You may sweat yet not have body odour. Or you may have body odour without a trace of sweat. It is very popular in India (especially with Indian males). Some say more popular than cricket.

Most of us will be able to recall our first meeting with body odour. Mine was when I bumped into our neighbour Mr Prakash. Although I was eight at the time, I immediately aged two years in just two minutes. Mr Prakash and I were in the building lift when the electricity mysteriously went off. Mr Prakash immediately went into a state of panic, which seemed to result in a certain emission of all his weapons of mass destruction. Except there was no mass present at the time, only a bewildered little boy. The body odour first came out slowly, as if it was watching the bowling and negotiating the pitch and watching the bounce and movement that the pitch had on offer. Then, as a couple of minutes passed without electricity, the body odour attacked.

Most of you will recall that body odour attacks in a collective strategic manner and tries to ensnare and constrict its victim. It is in this third stage, when the victim feels the body odour strangling away his life, that body odour's shape and form first becomes visible. As I watched the agitated Mr Prakash crumbling under pressure, it was clear

219

that he was summoning his entire body odour arsenal in an all-out assault with a clear mandate to take no prisoners. And, you must all remember this: you cannot negotiate with body odour. These guys don't fool around. They are the real killers, and in it to the death.

Coming back to the incident, as I felt the ghastly odour wearing me down, I too saw body odour's physical shape…err…take shape. The body odour was white with a light transparent top and an even tighter, more ill-fitting bottom. He seemed to have a permanent sneer on his ghostly white visage.

The thing about body odour's technique is that, while he's wearing you down, he's also shutting down your system. Your other senses start drying up and collapsing. Hearing, for example, becomes impaired, sight soon becomes questionable, and taste very quickly ceases to exist.

Just as I was about to accept my death by body odour, fate brought the electricity back and the lift opened its doors.

I never saw Mr Prakash again. Actually that's not true. I did see him again, but I declined to be within 75 feet of him. For me, it would always remain one of life's big contradictions. His name was Prakash, which means light. Yet it was not light, but smell which brought him into the…err…light.

Author's note: At the time of writing, 2:35 am, Monday, December 1, 2010, no cure for body odour has been found. Along with baldness, ageing, and marriage, it continues to be irreversible.

Dalal (not the kind you think)

When Mr Dalal actually died, nobody seemed surprised, least of all Mrs Dalal, the primary suspect. This was surprising to me because Mr Dalal was only 59 years old. But to everyone else Mr Dalal's death seemed inevitable, no, compulsory.

Mr Dalal, of course, wasn't always dead. In fact, in the few years I knew and observed him, I'd have to put my hand up and say he was very much alive.

He was the loudest and the most competitive man the world has seen since Genghis Khan. He was also a swimming father (Note: A swimming father is not a father who actually swims; in fact, in all probability he doesn't know how to swim, actually he is a father whose child is forced to swim and swim and swim by him). Of course, one is not sure if G. Khan was a swimming father.

Mr Dalal had three children. His intention was to have two. But when his neighbours, the Dasguptas, sprung a surprise and popped out a third kid, he promptly sent Mrs Dalal into labour so that they could keep up. Mr Dalal's kids were called Avneet, Alia, and Apeksha. All three were forced into the water at an early age. Primarily because Mr Dalal's elder brother had a daughter who was being written about in the sports pages for her backstroke prowess. And to this, Mr Dalal reacted in a very mature way. He removed the sports section from his regular morning paper and made sure it wound up in the dustbin. He would carry on with this practice even when he happened to visit his brother.

Once Mr Dalal started taking the kids for swimming practice, he quickly made an impression. This was not hard to do when you were the only parent trying to drown the other kids so that your kid has a better chance of winning the race. If one of his kids actually won a race, Mr Dalal would jump up and down, making faces and screaming obscenities. This by itself was not so bad. The problem was when he did this to the mother of the child who came second. If his child failed to win, he'd still do the exact same thing (jumping up and down and shouting obscenities), but this time the target of his performance would be his own child.

During diving practice, Mr Dalal would constantly shout words of encouragement. He would scream out words like 'pull' and 'push' at the top of his lungs. No one dared tell him that it was scientifically impossible to pull and push at the same time. Due to his unparalleled loudness, Mr Dalal soon got a nickname—'PD'. PD stood for 'Pushy Dalal'. No one ever called him this to his face because if they did, 'pushy' would quite naturally lead to 'shovy'.

Mr Dalal's wife, Amrita was the perfect foil to him. She would sit outside the swimming pool absolutely still and quite. She was so still a person that quiet often passersby would call for medical help, thinking her to be dead. However, Mrs Dalal would just sit there like an extra swimming bag till Mr Dalal said it was time to go home. Of the three kids, Avneet and Apeksha were quite ordinary at swimming and rarely won anything. This meant they were constantly being screamed at. This also explained why they continued to wear their ear plugs long after the swimming practice ended. Alia, on the other hand, was a real champion. She won everything in sight. Naturally she was highly favoured, and soon Avneet and Apeksha were reduced to carrying her bags to and from the practice sessions. Avneet and Apeksha didn't mind this as long as they could continue to keep their ear plugs in.

One fine day, when Alia won a closely contested race, PD started his usual acrobatics in front of the mother whose child had come in second. As he carried out his third jump and simultaneous fourth obscenity, PD fell into the pool clutching his chest. He never made it out of there alive. Of course, no one will ever know if he was alive for a time under water, as no one moved and no one reacted. Mrs Dalal seemed even more still than before. Apeksha and Avneet blamed it on the ear plugs. Alia was in the shower, and the rest of the swimming fraternity just waited and held its collective breath till its prayers were answered.

Later, when Mr Dalal was pronounced dead, no one actually celebrated openly, but no one seemed surprised.

The next day a strange phenomenon occurred—Mrs Dalal was seen…moving.

225

Powder puff boys

Do you know what separates us Indians from all other nationalities? In a word—powder. Okay, and it's not necessarily talcum powder. In fact, it's powder in absolutely any form. There is, of course, only one compulsory burning thing and that is that the powder must be white. White is the only hue powder really has to follow in order to thrive in India.

Let's understand it though, so that none of you start ringing me for clarifications about powder also being used in other parts of the world. In China, for instance, powder is often added into food, and may I tell you that in certain parts of Central America, powder is the food. The only food. The staple diet. All nine courses. I think you get the picture.

However, nowhere in the world has powder got the same following as in India. The manufacturers of powder in India are all in the *Forbes* 500 list. Most of them make the top fifty. Many have often offered to buy Forbes. But what makes powder so compelling a product? The answer goes back to the three most beautiful words in all literature— 'long, long, ago'.

Powder was discovered by the Persian king Darius the Great. Well, Darius the Great didn't personally discover powder because he was too busy waging war, and counting the bodies in his harem. Powder was actually discovered by Darius' court during their Friday executions. Every Friday, Darius would watch over the public executions of criminals, traitors, and any accessible passerby. The convicted would kneel face down while the heaviest camel would land a huge hoof on his head. Normally, this would take the camel thirty to forty attempts. In other words, fun for the whole family. Now, due to the gold plated hoofs, a certain gold dust residue would be left at the site.

This was the first, or rather prototype, of today's powder. What has this got to do with India? Well, for god's sake, if you'll only stop interrupting me, I'll tell you. Towards the end of his reign, somewhere in the musky fourth century BC, Darius crossed the Indus and arrived in the sub-continent. As he subjugated the locals left and right, Darius found

227

the climate totally insensible. Three things affected him badly, which he chronicles in his book *Darius, The Later Years*. Chapter Eight is devoted to India and is aptly titled, 'Never Again!'

a) his beautiful locks started falling. Or as the locals termed it, hairfall

b) he was forced to leave his mark all over the Indian countryside because of his incessant use of the portable toilets. Or as the locals like to call it, diarrhoea

c) he got his first pimple. Or as the locals like to call it, acne.

The first two seemed incurable, but for the third, Darius' doctor administered gold dust powder and it became an instant hit with both the Persians and the local population. Thus, trade between India and Persia was established. They gave us gold dust powder, and we gave them acne.

Powder caught on like crazy. Locals from the fourth century BC went on to say, on record, that the powder craze could only be matched by the Beatle mania. (And don't forget the Beatles weren't averse to using a little powder themselves).

Gold, obviously, was not to be the only source of powder. Other metals and soon new elements were discovered, and not all these new discoveries occurred during executions.

Today, we Indians use powder for many reasons. Those of a darker hue incessantly administer liberal doses of powder to whiten their skin. This is actually effective for exactly the amount of time the powder stays on the body, which is generally three and a half seconds or less. Others use it to curb itching—arguably India's greatest epidemic, which finally scared away many invaders from Darius to Timur, and later on George V as well. And though there is no conclusive link between the lessening of itching and the application of powder, this practice continues to grow.

There are also other lesser known functions of this master element. In parts of the south, powder is applied daily to trees to make them look a lot younger. Since the trees aren't able to protest, this act is not going to be curtailed anytime soon. In parts of the east, fish are showered in powder in an effort to help their reproductive capacity. This causes two reactions: the human population is happy it's done its good deed of the day, while the fish, for their part, sick of the ridicule, promptly head west to hopefully safer waters.

In the north, certain communities take this even further. During the rite of consummation, newlyweds apply the powder on the appropriate body parts to enhance their pleasure. While the women generally get it right, the men often read the script a little wrong and more often than not, powder their shoulders in an absolutely futile effort, which in all probability mirrors their future life together. All over the country, kids on their way to school are powdered from head to toe and then sent on their way. Parents may forget a tie, a belt, a sash or even shoes, but never ever powder.

In an ancient survey by Shah & Sons, it was found that every single Indian had, at one time or another, applied powder. This is a world record. One of which we all should be proud. All hail Darius, king of kings, and...err...king of... err...powder.

230

Drinking problem (not the inebriating kind)

As we reach the second decade of the twenty-first century (or is it twenty-second century, I really should check that), one thing seems abundantly certain, and that is the people of the world, civilization itself, will be divided on two lines. Yup, just two sides will split all of us. You either belong to the one side or to the other. As Mahesh said in Act III Scene V, or maybe George Bush in Act II, you are either with us or against us. So imagine that! The whole world divided into just two teams? And now it's time for the grand announcement. The two teams will be Team One—those who drink tea and Team Two—those who drink coffee. Now, nowhere will this divide be more prominent and derisive than in this little quaint village we all call home, namely India.

There are many permutations involved in the Indian beverage war. Let's take a look back. Tea was discovered in India 1,900 years ago in present-day Assam by a guy called Irani, who then went on to have a super successful career with the Tatas. Irani then went on to discover fiat and rubber, and was just about to discover plastic when on one dark night he was rolled over by a steamroller that was driving too slowly to be avoided. Tea became an instant hit with the citizens of India who today are known as Indians. For the next 1,600 years, tea held sway over our people. There simply was no challenger to this beverage of the Gods. Nimbu pani tried and failed. Sugarcane juice was forced to retire. Kala khatta put up a brave fight but all to no avail. Tea just rolled over them. Even in the north, where milk and lassi reigned, tea appeared and lassi became the bridesmaid. Milk had to be content with minors and really short adults. Everywhere you looked it was tea, tea, tea, and more tea for 1,600 years. And then, suddenly, like a meteor from the sky, coffee exploded on the Indian landscape.

The first NRI, one Hari Prasad, returned from New York in 1703 with three packets of, you guessed it, coffee. Immediately Hari Prasad's parents separated. Once exposed to coffee, Hari

Prasad's mom wanted to serve and consume only the latter. However, her husband Rishi Pal, a conservative traditionalist if ever there was one, a man who hadn't done a single thing differently in the past twenty-six years, wanted his regular tea. The lure of the two beverages meant that the first coffee-tea war was enacted in the Prasad house. Mrs Prasad won. She did this by pouring hot tea over Mr Rishi Prasad's head, thus destroying his precious hairstyle forever.

Meanwhile coffee started spreading its tentacles and spread in all four directions. However, its largest fan base was in the south. Tea, likewise, could always look at the east for formidable support. In just three hundred years, coffee has gained lots of ground, and though not yet undisputed, is poised to knock tea off its feet. Who will win this civilization's last great war?

I'll leave that to the beverage critics. Let me instead guide you to the logical differences in the makings of a coffee drinker vis-à-vis a tea drinker. So you know where you stand. And remember, you may consume both, but your love, your real passion, will only be for one.

Coffee drinkers are normally taller, wear white-coloured pants and prefer formal footwear. They are said to be dynamic and real bundles of energy.

Tea drinkers prefer pastels, dark shades, and the occasional manoeuvers. They tend to be quite refined, sophisticated, and rarely in a hurry. A coffee drinker is far more likely to attempt to pat a tiger in the wild, and a tea drinker, on the other hand, is more likely to ignore the tiger. This probably explains why there is a slightly higher number of tea drinkers than coffee drinkers in the world today.

Of course, in India we have an even more complex situation than elsewhere. As always, the caste system has to have a parallel, and soil Beveragestan. Tea has her hierarchy. The blue bloods prefer green tea, the next lot in rank go for masala chai, and the rabble exist on what is known as cutting chai. The term of course has nothing at all to do with the tea; instead, it refers to the cut you may have to endure from the cheap, often cracked glasses in which the chai is served.

Coffee drinkers have so many categories that it's almost impossible to mention them all. Suffice it to say that the higher classes are all well versed in Italian.

Next time you hear the phrase 'coffee, tea or me', remember to ignore it. There's really no question of me. Either you are tea, or you are coffee.

234

In Concludo!

Let me be straight up with you here. 'In Concludo' is deeply inspired by Oscar Wilde's *De Profundis*. With one major distinction and that is, while Oscar wrote his with a quill, I used a pink ball pen (which in any case I thought was very Oscar). Also, 'De Profundis' is definitely a legitimate phrase while 'In Concludo' is a made-up term not lawfully acceptable in any of the world's major languages.

First and second most, may I say that most of the valuable insights featured have personally occurred to or around me. The letters featured are all real, although the letter writer's identity may be fictitious, of course not in all cases, probably in only about 90 percent of them.

This book is not to be read by people under the age of 5. It is not advised if you are heavily, frequently lactating or suffering from any psychiatric disease. It is not be used to treat or cure any disease or illness, and, this above all, it must be wholly consumed in not more than four or five sittings.

The book by and large has three basic aims. One is to open the eyes of the general public to the habits and nature of the Indian male. Two, to help you pass time, and three, and this is the most noble reason, to ensure the publisher makes money.

People often ask me, why talk of only the Indian male, why not males of the entire world? My reply to these people has always been the same: 'Mind your own business'. Besides the only real difference between the Indian male and the World male is that Indian males are shorter.

Also, I'm attempting to write a book without much mention of Bollywood or cricket. This has never been done before by an Indian in India, not since Manu wrote his code of laws without many a mention of either modern day phenomena. For this, my courage and recklessness must be applauded. I'm also currently working on a musical version of this book, which should be ready for the market by the spring of 2016.

I must add here that I am not a member of the Al Qaeda, the LET, nor am I a long since suffering member of the Nazi party.

There are also quite a few topics that I haven't been able to touch with regard to Indian men. This may be due to rushed deadlines, but in all probability was caused by sheer boredom, and the repetitive nature of the topic. So I am enclosing a few empty pages so that the readers may freely complete my masterpiece by themselves, on their own time.

As keeping with the times, not a single paisa from the sales of this book will go to charity. Thus, feel free to buy more than one copy. Also please note, all grammatical mistakes and incomplete

237

sentences are intentional, so desist from making your own corrections; such an act will only make me mad. And the consequence of the anger is I'll need to write another book.

Coming to the Indian male. May I begin by saluting him, and now with my hand as well. This book is not meant to bring him down. It is, in fact, an instrument to bring him 'out'. Let him not go down the way of the Lochness monster, and the abominable snowman. Society today malfunctions because of ignorance. Knowledge and openness is the only form of redressal. Since much of the time I have been a card-carrying Indian male, I hope the book is not seen as an act of betrayal, rather I hope it's seen as an act of spreading awareness.

As I conclude 'In Concludo', I would like to quote from *Macbeth*. Unfortunately, I haven't read *Macbeth*, so that is an exercise in futility.

To all the wonderful Indian women I will say this, after reading this piece of literature, if they could put the book down, and say 'Thank God! We weren't born men', my job will be said to have been done.

238

Epilogue (how writing this book has helped me)

I am still recovering. Let me just be frank. I am an animal lover. Always have been. So is my wife, otherwise she wouldn't have married me.

Yet being asked to be a spokesperson for animals is a big deal. Especially for the animals. I felt quite touched. I'll never forget the exact words on the phone line, 'Cyrus, it's a recession and we can't find any real celebrities this week, so you'll have to do.' What an honour! I was ecstatic. PETA had approached me. I hadn't approached them, mind you. PETA had, in an apparently acute fit of absolute desperation, approached me. Me!

The issue, of course, was monkeys. Monkeys held in captivity at AIIMS. And I don't mean the harmless monkeys being treated in the main hospital. In fact,

I really wish they'd put some of them in those cages. Instead, PETA organized a photo shoot, and I was to be the protester portrayed in the photograph, in support of the monkeys. Of course, and this is just between you and me, nobody bothered to tell the monkeys. But that's another story.

The location was at a studio in Byculla, South Mumbai. We entered a mill gate, and then traversed a distance roughly the size of Pataliputra. In fact, I'm convinced it was Pataliputra because the ancient city of Pataliputra is one of very few cities in India that doesn't put up any signs. Outside the studio was a huge river. First I thought it was the Ravi; then I realized I was being facetious. The River Ravi? Of course not, it very clearly was the Chenab. A couple of kingfishers were visible near its bank. I knew immediately that they were kingfishers because there were no signs to say they weren't kingfishers.

The photographer, Himanshu, greeted me by laughing hysterically. This carried on for an hour. Then he was administered some Benadryl and fruitcake. He took too much. And everyone knows that too much fruitcake can kill you.

Himanshu declared himself fit for the shoot, but first he had to lie down. This, of course, led to more fruitcake and more Benadryl. After a two hour nap, Himanshu woke up and, feeling refreshed, he called for a wig. After putting on one that made him look like Celine Dion, he started the shoot. First he asked me to stand up. Not satisfied with this result, he then asked me to sit down. This continued until I pulled off his wig and begged him for many? This gave him a bright idea. He made me into Celine Dion and started clicking away.

Himanshu had devised three basic shots. In the first one, I enter his frame with both hands up and feet spread wide and off the ground. We tried explaining to him that this shot was only possible if you were a crow. Himanshu would hear none of it. He had .00563 of a second in terms of time while I held the pose, after which I hit the ground. We tried this twenty-six times, and each time I landed on a different body part. Some of which I hadn't visited in a while. But .00563 of a second is more than enough time if you're either an ace photographer or a germ. (In a germ's case, I'm told, .00563 of a second is half the germ's lifetime. This, of course, is in the event the germ has not been accidentally killed by, say, a speeding train or a misguided cough).

The second shot had me enact more idiotic poses. I strained every sinew, flexed every facial muscle and contoured every possible expression. However, Himanshu wasn't happy. He asked me to restrain myself and instead be perfectly still as he clicked away. After a few clicks he seemed satisfied, or so I gathered as he asked for more fruitcake and Benadryl, which was promptly delivered.

The third pose, I think, was devised with the possible connivance of my in-laws. I was to stand tall, all 5 feet 8 inches Celine Dion of me, with one finger from each hand immersed in an electric socket.

It soon became clear to me that Marconi was a complete liar, and Edison a fraud. Electricity had to have been discovered by Albert Einstein and maybe boxing promoter Don King. How else can you explain the hairstyle? Not only did I look like the bi-product of a relationship between Einstein and Don King (leaning more toward Mr King), the electric shock introduced into my body made everything numb except for my hair. Which means all my feeling was now in my hair alone. The hair itself stood on end like a commercial for Viagra gone wrong.

I don't know which of the three pictures PETA chose to display, but I do know that if he's watching from above, looking at those pictures, Darwin would be proud. His connection couldn't have been made clearer. Although he may want to reverse the order.

Acknowledgements

This book would not have been possible without the sustained and dramatic help of three very important people. Three people who are obviously very close to me. The only problem is I can't remember who they are, so if you are one of them please write in to Random House err ... randomly, and we will put your name in on our merit list, immediately.

I would like to acknowledge various influences that have shaped my philosophy over the years. Amongst them are Errol Flynn, Elvis Presley, and South African fast bowler Garth Le Roux and tall. Although it must be said, at 6 foot one inch, Elvis stood the tallest.

How can I not acknowledge the contribution of Anna Hazare. It is his sartorial sense and his sartorial sense alone that I follow today.

Sir Edmund Hillary, sorry make that Hillary Clinton, has also left her mark. I thank her most heartfully as well.

Next I must not forget my family try as I may. My sweet mother for dismissing my father for ignoring me. My wife for avoiding me and Mikhail and Maya for refusing to acknowledge me in public. And yes Ruffo, you as well.

I have three friends. Kunal, who is a professional smoker and who has written a note in the book; Vikram, who has no idea about this great Almonae; and Anup, who gave up reading at the age of 11 and a half years.

Finally, thank you...*aah*...reader for reading this passage and yes I will sign any pirated copy.

Above all my thanks to Milee at Random House who insisted on publishing this second book based on a famous scientific principle: that she has never bothered to read the first one.

In the words of a famous South Mumbai college: JAI HIND!

About the Author

The author was born many years ago, give and take a day. Over several decades he has refused to grow up.

A few facts about the author:
a) He was born left-handed, yet flosses and brushes with his right hand.
b) Has been a woman for seven years, but has lately changed his mind. (This is clearly a consequence of having been a lady for far too long).
c) Has tremendous influence and power within the higher echelons of Random House.
d) Has written the first four pages, as well as two paragraphs on page 37, all by himself.

Awards:
The author has won many awards, including the second prize in the potato race for class 2G in

Prakash
2/12/11

1980; The Royal Oalm, The Blue Diamond, and The Purple Rose of Cairo awards—all for casual conversation.

Inspiration:
Include Chekhov (not Anton but Dimitri), Cervantes (not Miguel but Manuel), and Bronte (not Emily but both her parents and their English Mastiff, Spot).